EVERYTHING YOU EVER WANTED TO KNOW ABOUT THE WORLD CUP

VOLUME ONE: 1930 – 1954

BY SAM BERKELEY

© Sam Berkeley 2013

All rights reserved.

First published in 2013

The moral right of the author has been asserted.

ISBN 978-1300912132

By the same author:

Everything You Ever Wanted To Know About the World Cup
Volume One: 1930-1954
Volume Two: 1958-1966
Volume Three: 1970-1978
Volume Four: 1982-1990
Volume Five: 1994-1998
Volume Six: 2002-2006
Volume Seven: 2010-2014 plus All-time World Cup Squads

CONTENTS

Foreword by Gary Lineker — 5

Introduction — 7

1930 Uruguay — 9

1934 Italy — 29

1938 France — 49

1950 Brazil — 71

1954 Switzerland — 93

FOREWORD

Playing in the World Cup is the peak of any player's career. Club football might have all the money and might take up the vast majority of the season, but the international game has something domestic football can never match: the ability to unite a country. To put on the national team shirt is what every boy dreams of as a child and in the international game there is nothing that compares to the World Cup.

I was lucky enough in my time as a player to go to two World Cups and I still treasure my experiences in those two tournaments more than any other moments in my footballing career. Of course in 1986 and 1990 there were both fabulous highs and unbearable lows, but that is what football, and in particular the World Cup, is all about. Winning the Golden Boot in '86 and finishing as the highest British goalscorer in World Cup history are records I treasure; but at the same time no moments haunt me like Maradona's two goals and that heartbreaking penalty shoot-out loss to the Germans four years later. To play in the World Cup is to go through a rollercoaster of emotions, just as is watching it on TV. Because it matters so much, because you know an entire country is urging you, begging you to win, that is why the World Cup remains the world's most popular sporting tournament.

The World Cup has made generation after generation fall in love with football. Even those who aren't footie fans the rest of the time can't help but be captivated by the gladiatorial spectacle which takes over the black box in the corner of every home every four years. Millions around the world will watch and wish they were on the pitch themselves. Only a tiny handful will ever achieve that lofty ambition, but those that do will have been inspired by those childhood dreams.

For the vast majority for whom playing in the competition forever remains a pipedream, they must find another way to get their World Cup fix. Watching game after game on TV, absorbing trivia and endlessly talking about the tournament to anyone who'll listen are just some of the ways a World Cup obsessed fan can maximise their own enjoyment of the competition. And of course when it comes to books there are a large number for the World Cup lover to choose from.

Most World Cup books fall into two categories: the encyclopaedia types full of facts and stats; and the passing guides, which give a general overview of the World Cup. There's little in between the two, nothing which gives the reader all the information in an accessible and entertaining way, nothing both comprehensive and easily readable.

Where this series of books delivers, and others fail, is in that middle ground. Each volume is packed full of all the facts and figures even the most ardent World Cup fan could ever need, with not a single game, in qualifying or the finals, ignored. From 1930 to 2010 every tournament is covered in the utmost detail. But it can also be picked up and enjoyed by someone with just a passing interest in the game, with interesting trivia – and some of the bizarre incidents which make the World Cup so special – highlighted to make it easier for the reader to get to the heart of the most interesting bits of each tournament.

Over the years, some of the greatest footballers to have ever played the game have graced the World Cup and given career-defining performances. No-one who ever saw them could forget Diego Maradona's mesmerizing displays in 1986, Pele's masterclass in 1970, or Ronaldo's predatory finishing in 2002. These legends are far from forgotten in this series too, featuring as it does brief biographies of some of the World Cup's all-time greatest players (from Jose Nasazzi to Carles Puyol, Gerd Muller to yours truly!) There's also a personal touch provided from the author, Sam Berkeley, with the selection of some personal all-time teams for the tournament's most successful nations. Debates over great players and teams can go on forever and these selections are sure to add plenty more fuel to the fire!

Even if the football in more recent tournaments hasn't always been of the highest standard, there is no doubt at all that the World Cup will still be holding millions around the world in its spell for decades to come. No matter what happens, football fans will always treasure it and count down the months and years before it is upon them once again. With this series of books you can make sure you're always prepared for and excited about the next instalment. And with your appetite whetted, the football itself will be even more enjoyable.

The World Cup has been a glorious crowd-pleaser for close on a century now. Long may it continue to be the pinnacle of every player's career. Here's to the next 100 years.

Gary Lineker

Introduction

"WHAT THE HELL WERE YOU THINKING?!" The living room exploded in a burst of fury as profanities were spat out and fingers jabbed in the direction of the little black box in the corner. "PLEASE DON'T SEND HIM OFF, PLEASE!" But it was too late. With an icy, emotionless stare the referee reached into the pocket of his garish red neon shirt and out came a flash of scarlet. Time seemed to slow down as realisation slowly dawned on the small semicircle enclosing the television. That was that. There was no hope. England were surely dead and buried now. David Beckham, my hero just a game before, was now the arch-villain of the household.

For me, the World Cup has always been the ultimate. As great as club football is, for all the thrills and spills of the Premiership, La Liga and the Champions League, nothing can touch the sheer passion and importance of the international game. Somehow when the pride of an entire nation is at stake, winning becomes so much more than a priority; it becomes a necessity. As a fresh-faced 11-year-old, France 98 captured my imagination in a way football had never done before. Religiously following England, I cheered against Tunisia, cried against Romania and was left with a strange mix of pride, rage and utter desolation after that Argentina game, Beckham's red card and penalty heartache. The world's most popular sporting competition has kept me held firmly in its grip ever since.

What makes the World Cup so great is all the subplots running through every fixture, from the earliest preliminaries in qualifying all the way to the final itself. The varying hopes and expectations of the contestants are all the more important when these contestants represent countries, where defeat can plunge a state into depression (and in the case of Argentina in 1930 even prompt a revolution!) and victory can revive an entire nation. For some it is merely the taking part that counts, for others anything but the trophy is a tragedy. The format allows for all sorts of intriguing possibilities. What happens when two weaker teams meet each other and have the rare chance of victory? What about when two of the games' giants clash and for both victory is not just clamoured for but demanded? And what about when the Davids meet the Goliaths and the intriguing possiblity of a monumental upset rears its head?

The World Cup is full of these intriguing storylines, every time throwing up results and events which even a fairytale writer would reject as too fanciful. Who would possibly have predicted that North Korea would beat Italy in 1966? That reigning champions France would not score a single goal in 2002? That a particularly bad-tempered qualifier in 1969 would prompt a full-scale war between Honduras and El Salvador? The World Cup captures the hearts and minds of people the world over precisely because it is so unpredictable and intriguing.

But more than anything else the World Cup is the pinnacle of football because it provides a nation with hopes and dreams of glory every four years. Through the good times and the bad the memories are surely the most vivid in football, be they the glory of 1966's triumph or the sorrow of 1990's penalty agony; Michael Owen's 1998 wonder goal against Argentina or Diego Maradona's own masterpiece for the other side back in 1986. Every country treasures the good and the bad in almost equal measure. After all, maybe next time will be our time…

This series of books is a detailed and comprehensive history of the globe's most loved tournament. From its earliest beginnings and inauguration in the cold Uruguayan winter back in 1930 to its latest incarnation in Brazil 2014, no tournament is left uncovered. Here is every goal ever scored, both in qualifying and in the finals themselves, every controversy, every ugly confrontation, every glorious triumph, every iconic moment, every piece of unforgettable football genius. Any question you could possibly have about the World Cup is answered here. Also included in the final book of the series are some all-time team selections for all the major contenders throughout its history – no facts there, just good old opinion, whether you agree with it or not! The best players, goals and starting XIs at the end of each World Cup tournament are also my own selections, rather than the often dubious ones picked by FIFA (Oliver Kahn over Ronaldo in 2002 anyone?). But that, of course, is just another reason why the World Cup is so great: for footie fans young and old it is an endless and much-loved talking point and the subject of constant debate. At least with this book you have all the facts and stats you need to hold your own in the unforgiving world that is World Cup chitchat! For decades to come the World Cup will continue to entice, delight, frustrate and elate in equal measure. I hope you, like me, will always treasure every moment.

1930: Uruguay

13 Entrants.

Uruguay, **Argentina**, **Chile**, **Brazil**, **Bolivia**, **Peru**, **Paraguay**, **Mexico**, **USA**, **France**, **Yugoslavia**, **Romania** and **Belgium** qualified.

> **Stat Attack**
>
> The inaugural World Cup in 1930 was the only one not to feature a qualifying tournament. All 13 teams who entered qualified automatically.

The Contenders

Argentina	Paraguay
Belgium	Peru
Bolivia	Romania
Brazil	Uruguay
Chile	USA
France	Yugoslavia
Mexico	

The World Cup first came about thanks to the passion and drive of the FIFA President at the time, Frenchman Jules Rimet. With the advent of professionalism, it was considered that the amateur football competition in the Olympic Games, recognised by FIFA as the official world championship in the 1920s, was no longer truly representative of the game as a whole. On May 26

1928, the World Cup was established at the FIFA Congress in Amsterdam, with its members voting overwhelmingly in favour.

Several countries offered to host the first World Cup, most of them European. Among them were Sweden, perhaps surprisingly, as they had actually been one of the few associations who had voted against the tournament! Nevertheless, they, together with Spain, Holland, Hungary and Italy, expressed their desire to host the new tournament. However, in the end these nations all withdrew from the bidding process, instead letting the World Cup go to Uruguay, Olympic champions in 1924 and 1928, who would be celebrating a hundred years of independence in 1930, when the competition would take place. They were building a brand new stadium, the Centenario, in the capital Montevideo to mark the event and host the final. It would be one of three stadiums, all in Montevideo, to host matches in the tournament.

Although all member associations agreed on the choice of Uruguay as hosts, inevitably the difficulties of travelling to South America were to have a severely detrimental effect on the tournament, since they resulted in Europe's best sides declining to attend. Indeed, not a single European side had entered two months prior to the start of the tournament, even though the Uruguayans extended them the kind gesture of offering to pay all their travel costs. Again, it would be Rimet to the rescue, eventually ensuring the participation of four European sides: France, Belgium, Romania and Yugoslavia. None were among the top tier of the continent's footballing hierarchy, however, and there were fears that they would be no match for the South Americans, especially after weeks of travel by boat, when they would be unable to train properly, a far cry from the fastidious pre-tournament preparations seen nowadays.

Nevertheless, at least Europe would be one of three continents represented at the tournament, joining teams from North and South America. The 13 entrants were divided into four groups, one of four and three of three. The teams would play each other once each, with the group winners advancing to the semi-finals. The prize awaiting the tournament victors would be the cup which would later become known as the Jules Rimet Trophy, in honour of the FIFA President's instrumental role in bringing about the competition. Sculpted by Abel Lafleur, it depicted Nike, the Greek goddess of victory, with arms held aloft in celebration.

Argentina, runners-up to Uruguay in the 1928 Olympics, were the seeds and most fancied side in Group One. Their side was based around rugged centre half Luis Monti, while promising young centre forward Guillermo Stabile looked a great goal-scoring prospect. Opposing them in the group would be **France**, who could consider themselves the founders of the competition. In inside forward Edmond Delfour and goalkeeper Alex Thepot they had quality players but few expected their largely average team to be capable of competing with the Argentineans. **Chile** too would have a chance, playing close to home and building a good reputation for their football. Their key men would be inside forwards Guillermo Subiabre and Carlos Vidal. Group One also featured a fourth side in **Mexico**, newcomers to the international game and big outsiders. There were fears that they could be on the end of a massacre.

Heading up Group Two were seeds **Brazil**. With such a large and football-mad populace, they would be dangerous, though they were yet to establish themselves as a real force on the international scene and were certainly not a team of the quality of their Uruguayan and Argentinean neighbours. Racism also remained an issue in their selection policies, with many of the country's best black players routinely ignored. At least in forward Preguinho they had a cutting edge. Their chief rivals for a semi-final place would likely be **Yugoslavia**, who looked the best of the four European sides present. They boasted quality professionals in centre half Ljubisa Stefanovic, winger Branislav Sekulic and centre forward Ivan Bek, while 18-year-old right winger Aleksandar Tirnanic would also carry a potent threat. **Bolivia**, completing the group, were unfancied and believed to be no more than cannon fodder for the group's other two teams.

Hosts and favourites **Uruguay** would play in Group Three. They would be without brilliant goalkeeper Andres Mazali, who had starred in the team's Olympic triumphs, after he broke a team curfew but coach Alberto Suppici could call upon an array of talent. Captain and right-back Jose Nasazzi was a commanding defender who was also instrumental in launching attacks from the back; right half Jose Leandro Andrade, one of football's first black stars, was a formidable shield in the centre of the field who had creative ability too; veteran inside right Hector Scarone was a hugely talented playmaker and regular goalscorer; and the experienced Pedro Cea and Pedro Petrone would provide cutting edge up front. **Romania** would be one of the sides tasked with stopping the hosts. The "King's Men" had a fine centre half in Emerich Vogl but few gave them a prayer against Uruguay. **Peru** too would have the daunting task of facing the Uruguayans and they were even bigger outsiders in the group.

Group Four's seeded side were the **USA**, on the basis of their new professional league, though they were hardly among the heavyweights of world football, especially as the sport was not particularly popular in the country. Forward Tom Florie, a star of the American Soccer League, would look to show off his ability and the Americans would certainly not lack fitness with their professional league. Indeed, the French dubbed them "the shot-putters" in reference to their considerable athletic training. Their opponents would include **Belgium**, not highly regarded back in Europe, though Bernard Voorhoof was a prolific striker. **Paraguay** would challenge the other two sides in Group Four. They boasted a formidable forward line, including several of the early-day greats of South American football, such as Aurelio Gonzalez, Delfin Benitez Caceres and Luis Vargas Pena, all dangerous players. They would be the team to beat in the group.

> **Only at the World Cup**
>
> Uruguay's star keeper Andres Mazali was dismissed from the squad after breaking a curfew, sneaking out to see his family!

> **Only at the World Cup**
>
> Romania's football-mad monarch King Carol II was so eager for his team to take part in the 1930 World Cup that he picked the team himself and liaised with their clubs to allow them to play in the tournament while still receiving pay! Somehow I can't imagine David Cameron confronting Sir Alex Ferguson in quite the same manner!

Debutants: Argentina, Belgium, Bolivia, Brazil, Chile, France, Mexico, Paraguay, Peru, Romania, Uruguay, USA, Yugoslavia

The Draw

Group 1
Argentina
Chile
France
Mexico

Group 2
Brazil
Bolivia
Yugoslavia

Group 3
Uruguay
Peru
Romania

Group 4
USA
Belgium
Paraguay

Venues:
Montevideo – Centenario, Parque Central, Pocitos

Only at the World Cup

The Centenario had been intended to host all the games but it was only finished in time for the last ten matches. There's Uruguayan builders for you!

The Tournament – 13-30 July

Group Stage – First series

The first ever World Cup games were played simultaneously on the 13th July. While the USA were playing Belgium at Parque Central, **France** took the game to **Mexico** at the Estadio Pocitos in front of a measly 3,000 fans (though some reports suggest the crowd was even smaller), as the Uruguayan public seemed remarkably disinterested. The conditions were not conducive to football, as France inside forward Lucien Laurent later revealed that there was snow falling as the match took place! Nevertheless, the Europeans wasted no time in sweeping aside their inferior opponents, Laurent volleying in the first ever World Cup goal to put them ahead after 19 minutes. France suffered a blow five minutes later when goalkeeper Alex Thepot was forced off injured.

Stat Attack

Rather fittingly, as the French had been the creators of the tournament, it was a Frenchman, Lucien Laurent, who scored the first ever goal at a World Cup.

With substitutions not to be permitted for a further 40 years, right half Augustin Chantrel went between the sticks, with the side forced to play on with ten men. Nevertheless, the French were three up before half-time, Laurent's fellow forwards Marcel Langiller and Andre Maschinot stretching their lead. The Central Americans made things harder for their opponents in the second period and got themselves on the scoresheet through Juan Carreno, who two years earlier had also been the scorer of Mexico's first ever goal at the Olympics. France were to add a fourth late on, however, Maschinot the man on target. It was a fine start for the French and suggested the European sides shouldn't be written off in the tournament just yet.

Meanwhile, France's neighbours **Belgium** were shocked by a powerful and skilful **USA** team. With a team full of players originating from Britain but who played in the American Soccer League, they tore the outclassed Belgians apart, leaving them chasing shadows with their greater speed, strength and movement. However, the scores were level until just before half-time, when Scottish-born winger Bart McGhee scored a quick-fire double, the second of which angered the Belgians, as they believed it to be offside. However, they were unable to fashion a response in the second half, centre forward Bert Patenaude scoring a late third. The US had won impressively, much to the surprise of the Uruguayan public and the rest of the world.

The following day, **Yugoslavia** caused another shock by deservedly beating **Brazil**. The Brazilians' preparations had been spoiled by a spat between their federation, based in Rio de Janeiro, and the clubs in Sao Paulo, resulting in several of their best players not travelling. Nevertheless, they had still been expected to win but the lively Yugoslavs had other ideas. The freezing cold of the Uruguayan winter affected the Brazilians' play and their opponents took advantage. 18-year-old Tirnanic briefly became the youngest World Cup goalscorer with the Eastern Europeans' first goal and the dangerous Ivan Bek soon doubled their advantage. The Brazilians, desperate to fight back, poured forward in the second period but one goal, scored by their captain Preguinho, was scant consolation. The Yugoslav defence, with centre half Ljubisa Stefanovic at the heart, performed heroically to deny the South Americans time and again and Brazil's World Cup hopes had been dealt a severe blow.

Later that day, a miniscule crowd of 300 people watched **Romania** also get one over a South American side, battling to victory over **Peru**. The game sparked into life after a matter of seconds, Adalbert Desu putting the Europeans in front. From then on, the match descended into ugly scenes, with numerous fouls being committed by both sides. The Peruvians, the chief offenders, found themselves down to ten men early in the second half, half-back Placido Galindo sent off for a foul on opposite number Ladislau Raffinsky amid more violent scenes. Nevertheless, the outnumbered Peruvians fought back and surprisingly levelled, Luis Souza Ferreira scoring a surprise equaliser. However, the Romanians were eventually to make their numerical advantage count, Stefan Barbu and Constantin Stanciu scoring late on for a final score of 3-1.

> **Only at the World Cup**
>
> All but one of the Brazilian players present at the 1930 World Cup were from Rio clubs, after Sao Paulo managers were passed over for selecting the team. They responded by refusing to release their players from the clubs, with the exception of Santos striker Araken, who decided to break ranks and play anyway.

> **Stat Attack**
>
> The 300 people who watched Romania beat Peru 3-1 is the smallest crowd ever at the World Cup finals.

> **Stat Attack**
>
> Peru's Placido Galindo was the first player ever sent off at a World Cup.

Group Stage – Second series

Next up was **Argentina**'s clash with **France**, surprisingly, since it would be France's second game of the tournament and only Argentina's first, while Chile were still to play their first match! Nevertheless, the two sides played out an ugly and bad-tempered game. The key figure in the match was Argentina's uncompromising centre half Luis Monti, who stopped the French forwards both by fair means and foul but was superb in dominating the game, while releasing his own forwards with raking, accurate passes. It was Monti who scored the game's decisive goal, firing in a free-kick with ten minutes remaining. However, the game was to end in huge controversy. The French worked Langiller into a great shooting position but as he looked to pull the trigger, Brazilian referee Almeida Rego blew for full time, despite the fact it was only the 39th minute of the second half! After prolonged protests from the French, the game was restarted, but the chance had gone and the score remained the same to the end. France were understandably unhappy at their defeat, not helped by refereeing decisions or the questionable match schedule. This would not be the only organisational gaffe in the history of the World Cup.

> **Only at the World Cup**
>
> Referee Rego cost France the game against Argentina, blowing for full time six minutes early as they pressed for an equaliser! Eventually, he did decide to restart the game, though several players were already in the shower, but there was no further score.

Chile finally got a chance to show what they could do the following day and instantly took it, firing three past **Mexico**, who as against France were found willing but not able, lacking the necessary experience of international football to compete with their opponents over the course of 90 minutes. They were behind in the opening stages to Guillermo Subiabre's early goal. The inside right was a constant thorn in the Mexicans' side all game, adding a second before his inside forward partner Carlos Vidal made it three to eliminate the Central Americans.

Yugoslavia became the first team to qualify for the semi-finals, thumping the minnows of **Bolivia** 4-0. However, it was not all as plain sailing as the result might suggest. The South Americans exhibited no little passion and defensive commitment to frustrate the Europeans for an hour, with a draw looking a distinct possibility. However, eventually their resistance collapsed, broken by Ivan Bek's rapid double midway through the second half. Beaten, they fell apart and inside forwards Blagoje Marjanovic and Djordje Vujadinovic helped themselves to a goal each to complete the rout. The Yugoslavs had impressed again and were worthy semi-finalists.

The **USA** also had a chance to seal their participation in the last four by beating **Paraguay**. Much to everyone's surprise, they achieved it, again showing the same power and pace that had left Belgium in tatters. Centre forward Bert Patenaude was the star, battering the Paraguayan defence and helping himself to a hat-trick, with captain Tom Florie's promptings also to the fore. The Americans had caused another shock, deservedly reaching the semi-finals, much to the surprise of their shell-shocked opponents.

> **Stat Attack**
>
> America's Bert Patenaude scored the first ever World Cup hat-trick against Paraguay.

> **Only at the World Cup**
>
> The 1930 World Cup had the strange quirk of the opening ceremony taking place in the middle of the tournament! Construction delays on the Centenario stadium postponed Uruguay's first game and the ceremony in honour of their centenary that accompanied it.

Hosts **Uruguay** finally entered the tournament against **Peru**. They had originally planned to open the tournament but the Centenario stadium had not been finished in time. Now it was finally ready and from this point on, all the remaining games were played in the new stadium. After a pre-game ceremony, the action finally got underway. Uruguay, backed by a huge and passionate home crowd, struggled with the great weight of expectation on their shoulders. They poured forward in search of goals but Peru, with an altered line-up from their defeat to Romania, refused to be breached, new goalkeeper Jorge Pardon in particular defiant in denying the hosts time and again. Finally, however, Uruguay did sneak a winner, Hector Castro with a good finish to give the hosts maximum points from their first game. There was no doubt they would have to radically improve, however, if they had ambitions of winning the tournament on home soil.

Group Stage – Third series

After defeat to Argentina, **France** had to beat **Chile** to have any chance of reaching the semi-finals. However, it was the South Americans who dominated the game, with only the heroics of Alex Thepot in goal keeping them level, including saving Guillermo Saavedra's penalty after half an hour. However, he was finally beaten by the inspired Subiabre, having another impressive game, who headed past him to finally break the deadlock. The score remained 1-0 to the end and France, the fathers of the competition, were out. They would now face the long journey back home across the ocean.

Mexico would have much less distance to cover on their return home but nevertheless, that was their destination after another heavy defeat, this time at the hands of **Argentina**. The Argentineans made several changes to the side that had been fortunate to beat France. Two of the players brought in, striker Guillermo Stabile and half-back Adolfo Zumelzu, helped themselves to five goals in the game, three for Stabile and two for Zumelzu. The match was also notable for featuring three penalties, thanks largely to the inept refereeing of Ulises Saucedo, who was also the Bolivian coach! The first was missed by Argentina full-back Fernando Paternoster before Mexico's Manuel Rosas scored the first successful World Cup penalty kick. Rosas would also have a second chance from the spot and although Angel Bossio saved his initial kick, he scored from the follow-up. Boca Juniors legend Francisco Varallo and Mexico's Roberto Gayon also got their names on the scoresheet in this 6-3 thriller. The victory, though, gave the South Americans an excellent chance of reaching the semi-finals.

The following day saw two matches that were now meaningless, since Yugoslavia and the USA had already ensured their progress. First up was **Brazil**'s meeting with **Bolivia**. As against Yugoslavia, the Bolivians resisted bravely

> **Only at the World Cup**
>
> The referee for Argentina's clash with Mexico ludicrously was Bolivia's coach Ulises Saucedo! Unsurprisingly, he proved a controversial figure in the match, awarding three dubious penalties. Maybe Arsene "I didn't see it" Wenger would have been more lenient!

> **Stat Attack**
>
> As well as being the first player to score a penalty in a World Cup, Mexico's Manuel Rosas became the youngest ever World Cup goalscorer, a record he would eventually relinquish to Pelé in 1958.

> **Only at the World Cup**
>
> The opening 45 minutes of the Brazil-Bolivia game were farcical, as both teams were playing in the same colour kit! Eventually, the Bolivians changed at half-time.

15

in the first half, perhaps helped by the confusion over the colour clash of the sides' kits, with Moderato scoring the only goal of the opening period. After the break, with normality restored to the teams' appearance, the Brazilians found their feet and scored a further three times, Preguinho notching two and Moderato also claiming his second. The Bolivians had fought bravely but had been outclassed again while Brazil, although impressive victors, would also go home.

Meanwhile, **Belgium** and **Paraguay** also sought a consolation victory before they too departed. The game was settled by a goal by the South Americans' star winger, Luis Vargas Pena, condemning the Belgians to another depressing defeat. They, like the Bolivians, would exit the tournament without a goal to their name. The Paraguayans had some small consolation but it was all in vain and they would be going home also.

Uruguay, slated by their press after their unconvincing victory over Peru, went into their Group Three game with **Romania** needing to win. They had made four changes to the side who had struggled through their opening game, bringing Ernesto Mascheroni into the left-back position ahead of Domingo Tejera, preferring the versatile Pablo Dorado on the right wing ahead of Olympics veteran Santos Urdinaran, and freshening up the forward line with veteran Hector Scarone and Peregrino Anselmo replacing Hector Castro and Pedro Petrone. With this new-look side, the hosts swept over the bewildered Romanians, linking up gorgeously in attack to score four first-half goals, newcomers Dorado, Scarone and Anselmo all on target together with veteran Pedro Cea. Despite their domination, they were unable to add to their lead in the second period but they were comfortably through to the semi-finals and this much-improved performance had their fans dreaming of lifting the World Cup in the same stadium nine days later.

The last match of the first round was the Group One clash between **Argentina** and **Chile**, both of whom had won their previous two games and so were chasing the last semi-final spot. The prolific newcomer to the Argentinean line-up, Guillermo Stabile set his side on their way with an early brace and though Guillermo Subiabre responded for Chile minutes later, an equaliser remained beyond them. Outside left Mario Evaristo consigned them to elimination with a third goal in the second half. Argentina had claimed the final spot in the semis at the expense of the Chileans, who had come up just short despite an impressive tournament.

First Round results

Group 1

France 4-1 Mexico
13/07/30 – Montevideo (Pocitos)
France: Thepot, Mattler, Capelle, Chantrel, Pinel, Villaplane (c), Liberati, Delfour, Maschinot, L Laurent, Langiller
Goals: L Laurent 19, Langiller 40, Maschinot 43, 87
Mexico: Bonfiglio, R Garza Gutierrez (c), M Rosas, Amezcua, Sanchez, F Rosas, Lopez, Ruiz, Mejia, Carreno, Perez
Goals: Carreno 70
Referee: Lombardi (Uruguay)

Argentina 1-0 France
15/07/30 – Montevideo (Parque Central)
Argentina: Bossio, Della Torre, Muttis, J Evaristo, Monti, Suarez, Perinetti, Varallo, Ferreira (c), Cherro, M Evaristo
Goals: Monti 81
France: Thepot, Mattler, Capelle, Chantrel, Pinel, Villaplane (c), Liberati, Delfour, Maschinot, L Laurent, Langiller
Referee: Rego (Brazil)

Chile 3-0 Mexico
16/07/30 – Montevideo (Parque Central)
Chile: Cortes, Poirier, Morales, A Torres, Saavedra, Elgueta, Ojeda, Subiabre, Villalobos, Vidal, Schneeberger (c)
Goals: Subiabre 3, 52, Vidal 65
Mexico: Sota, R Garza Gutierrez (c), M Rosas, Amezcua, Sanchez, F Rosas, Lopez, Gayon, Ruiz, Carreno, Perez
Referee: Christophe (Belgium)

Chile 1-0 France
19/07/30 – Montevideo (Centenario)
Chile: Cortes, Chaparro, Riveros, A Torres, Saavedra, C Torres, Ojeda, Subiabre, Villalobos, Vidal, Schneeberger (c)
Goals: Subiabre 65
France: Thepot, Mattler, Capelle, Chantrel, Delmer, Villaplane (c), Liberati, Delfour, Pinel, Veinante, Langiller
Referee: Tejada (Uruguay)

> **Only at the World Cup**
>
> Captaining his country in the 1930 World Cup was certainly the highlight of France half-back Alexandre Villaplane's career. The Algerian-born player would become involved in a brutal organisation which collaborated with the Nazis and murdered resistance fighters during the Second World War. After the Allies recaptured France, he was tried and executed as a war criminal in December 1944.

Argentina 6-3 Mexico
19/07/30 – Montevideo (Centenario)
Argentina: Bossio, Della Torre, Paternoster, Chividini, Zumelzu (c), Orlandini, Peucelle, Varallo, Stabile, Demaria, Spadaro
Goals: Stabile 8, 17, 80, Zumelzu 12, 55, Varallo 53
Mexico: Bonfiglio, R Garza Gutierrez (c), M Rosas, Olivares, Sanchez, Rodriguez, F Garza Gutierrez, F Rosas, Lopez, Gayon, Carreno
Goals: M Rosas pen 42, 65, Gayon 75
Referee: Saucedo (Bolivia)

Argentina 3-1 Chile
22/07/30 – Montevideo (Centenario)
Argentina: Bossio, Della Torre, Paternoster, J Evaristo, Monti, Orlandini, Peucelle, Varallo, Stabile, Ferreira (c), M Evaristo
Goals: Stabile 12, 13, M Evaristo 51
Chile: Cortes, Chaparro, Morales, A Torres, Saavedra (c), C Torres, Arellano, Subiabre, Villalobos, Vidal, Aguilera
Goals: Subiabre 15
Referee: Langenus (Belgium)

	Pld	W	D	L	GF	GA	Pts
Argentina	3	3	0	0	10	4	6
Chile	3	2	0	1	5	3	4
France	3	1	0	2	4	3	2
Mexico	3	0	0	3	4	13	0

Argentina qualified for semi-finals.

Group 2

Yugoslavia 2-1 Brazil
14/07/30 – Montevideo (Parque Central)
Yugoslavia: Jaksic, Ivkovic (c), Mihajlovic, Arsenijevic, Stefanovic, Djokic, Tirnanic, Marjanovic, Bek, Vujadinovic, Sekulic
Goals: Tirnanic 21, Bek 30
Brazil: Joel, Brilhante, Italia, Hermogenes, Fausto, Fernando, Poly, Nilo, Araken, Preguinho (c), Teophilo
Goals: Preguinho 62
Referee: Tejada (Uruguay)

Yugoslavia 4-0 Bolivia
17/07/30 – Montevideo (Parque Central)
Yugoslavia: Jaksic, Ivkovic (c), Mihajlovic, Arsenijevic, Stefanovic, Djokic, Tirnanic, Marjanovic, Bek, Vujadinovic, Najdanovic
Goals: Bek 60, 67, Marjanovic 65, Vujadinovic 85
Bolivia: Bermudez, Durandal, Chavarria, Argote, Lara, Valderrama, Gomez, Bustamante, Mendez (c), Alborta, Fernandez
Referee: Mateucci (Uruguay)

Brazil 4-0 Bolivia
20/07/30 – Montevideo (Centenario)
Brazil: Velloso, Ze Luiz, Italia, Hermogenes, Fausto, Fernando, Benedito, Russinho, Carvalho Leite, Preguinho (c), Moderato
Goals: Moderato 37, 73, Preguinho 57, 83
Bolivia: Bermudez, Durandal, Chavarria, Sainz, Lara, Valderrama, Ortiz, Bustamante, Mendez (c), Alborta, Fernandez
Referee: Balway (France)

	Pld	W	D	L	GF	GA	Pts
Yugoslavia	2	2	0	0	6	1	4
Brazil	2	1	0	1	5	2	2
Bolivia	2	0	0	2	0	8	0

Yugoslavia qualified for semi-finals.

Group 3

Romania 3-1 Peru
14/07/30 – Pocitos
Romania: Lapusneanu, Burger, A Steiner, Eisenbeisser, Vogl, Raffinsky, Covaci, Desu, Wetzer (c), Stanciu, Barbu
Goals: Desu 1, Barbu 85, Stanciu 85
Peru: Valdivieso, de las Casas, Soria, Galindo (c), Garcia, Valle, Lores, Villanueva, Denegri, Neyra, Souza Ferreira
Goals: Souza Ferreira 75
Sent off: Galindo 54
Referee: Warnken (Chile)

Uruguay 1-0 Peru
18/07/30 – Montevideo (Centenario)
Uruguay: Ballesteros, Nasazzi (c), Tejera, Andrade, Fernandez, Gestido, Urdinaran, Castro, Petrone, Cea, Iriarte
Goals: Castro 65
Peru: Pardon, de las Casas, Maquilon, Galindo (c), Denegri, Astengo, Lores, Villanueva, Lavalle, Neyra, Souza Ferreira
Referee: Langenus (Belgium)

Uruguay 4-0 Romania
21/07/30 – Montevideo (Centenario)
Uruguay: Ballesteros, Nasazzi (c), Mascheroni, Andrade, Fernandez, Gestido, Dorado, Scarone, Anselmo, Cea, Iriarte
Goals: Dorado 7, Scarone 26, Anselmo 31, Cea 35
Romania: Lapusneanu, Burger, Czako, Eisenbeisser, Vogl, Robe, Covaci, Desu, Wetzer (c), Raffinsky, Barbu
Referee: Rego (Brazil)

	Pld	W	D	L	GF	GA	Pts
Uruguay	2	2	0	0	5	0	4
Romania	2	1	0	1	3	5	2
Peru	2	0	0	2	1	4	0

Uruguay qualified for semi-finals.

Group 4

USA 3-0 Belgium
13/07/30 – Montevideo (Parque Central)
USA: Douglas, Wood, Moorhouse, Gallagher, Tracey, Auld, Brown, Florie (c), Patenaude, Gonsalves, McGhee
Goals: McGhee 41, 45, Patenaude 88
Belgium: Badjou, Nouwens, Hoydonckx, de Clerq, Hellemans, P Braine (c), Diddens, Voorhoof, Adams, Moeschal, Versijp
Referee: Macias (Argentina)

USA 3-0 Paraguay
17/07/30 – Montevideo (Parque Central)
USA: Douglas, Wood, Moorhouse, Gallagher, Tracey, Auld, Brown, Florie (c), Patenaude, Gonsalves, McGhee
Goals: Patenaude 10, 15, 50
Paraguay: Denis, Olmedo, Miracca, Etcheverry, Diaz, Aguirre, Nessi, Dominguez, Gonzalez, Benitez Caceres, Vargas Pena (c)
Referee: Macias (Argentina)

Paraguay 1-0 Belgium
20/07/30 – Montevideo (Centenario)
Paraguay: P Benitez, Olmedo, Flores, S Benitez, Diaz, Garcete, Nessi, Romero, Gonzalez, Benitez Caceres, Vargas Pena (c)
Goals: Vargas Pena 40
Belgium: Badjou, De Deken, Hoydonckx, Nouwens, Hellemans, P Braine (c), Diddens, Delbeke, Adams, Moeschal, Versijp
Referee: Vallarino (Uruguay)

	Pld	W	D	L	GF	GA	Pts
USA	2	2	0	0	6	0	4
Paraguay	2	1	0	1	1	3	2
Belgium	2	0	0	2	0	4	0

USA qualified for semi-finals.

Semi-finals

Argentina opened the semi-finals facing the **USA**, the tournament's surprise package. However, despite their impressive performances, no-one expected another US win, with the Argentines considered several steps above their previous opponents. So it proved in what was an astonishingly physical game. This was the sort of contest that the tough Luis Monti relished and it was him who opened the scoring midway through the first half. Monti and his team mates were delighting in getting stuck into the Americans, who, despite their incredible fitness levels, were picking up numerous injuries and would finish the game with just eight fit men on the field. The goals started to flow early in the second half, Alejandro Scopelli and Guillermo Stabile putting the South Americans in the driving seat. The game became a rout in the final ten minutes as the physically exhausted Americans fell apart in the face of the Argentineans' swift attacks, Carlos Peucelle scoring twice and Stabile also getting his second of the game before Jim Brown added a late consolation for the US. The Americans were unhappy with the brutal nature of the game but there was also little doubt that they had been thoroughly outclassed in footballing terms by the pace and movement of Argentina, who were clearly deserving of their place in the final.

> **Only at the World Cup**
>
> One of the most comical of all World Cup incidents occurred in the second half of the USA-Argentina match: the US trainer John Coll rushed onto the field to treat an injured player but in his haste dropped his bag, smashing a bottle of chloroform. Engulfed by the fumes, Coll collapsed and had to be carried off!

The second quarter-final was also to finish with the same 6-1 scoreline but was to follow a different pattern. Underdogs **Yugoslavia** took the lead in the opening minutes through Branislav Sekulic, shocking the mammoth crowd who had come to cheer on hosts **Uruguay**. Despite this setback, forwards Pedro Cea and Peregrino Anselmo pulled it back to 2-1 after 20 minutes. There was to be great controversy, however, as Yugoslavia thought they had equalised only for referee Rego, who had erred so crucially in the Argentina-France group game, to disallow it for a dubious offside. This was to prove the game's turning point as the incensed Europeans fell apart. Anselmo made it 3-1 before half-time, Santos Iriarte added a fourth on the hour before Cea scored twice late on to bag himself a hat-trick and complete a crushing victory. The only sour point for Uruguay was that Anselmo picked up an injury that would keep him out of the final. Nevertheless, the tens of thousands who had come to the Centenario to watch the game could reflect on money well spent. Next up would be Argentina in the final.

> **Only at the World Cup**
>
> US wing half Andy Auld, who had his lip torn open during the game, played much of the second half with a rag stuffed in his mouth to stem the bleeding! Now that's some high-tech physio work!

> **Stat Attack**
>
> Yugoslavia's trio of Ljubisa Stefanovic, Ivan Bek and Branislav Sekulic, who played for French clubs, were the only players in the tournament to ply their trade outside their home country.

Semi-final results

Argentina 6-1 USA
26/07/30 – Montevideo (Centenario)
Argentina: Botasso, Della Torre, Paternoster, J Evaristo, Monti, Orlandini, Peucelle, Scopelli, Stabile, Ferreira (c), M Evaristo
Goals: Monti 20, Scopelli 56, Stabile 69, 87, Peucelle 80, 85
USA: Douglas, Wood, Moorhouse, Gallagher, Tracey, Auld, Brown, Florie (c), Patenaude, Gonsalves, McGhee
Goals: Brown 89
Referee: Langenus (Belgium)

Uruguay 6-1 Yugoslavia
27/07/30 – Montevideo (Centenario)
Uruguay: Ballesteros, Nasazzi (c), Mascheroni, Andrade, Fernandez, Gestido, Dorado, Scarone, Anselmo, Cea, Iriarte
Goals: Cea 18, 67, 72, Anselmo 20, 31, Iriarte 61
Yugoslavia: Jaksic, Ivkovic (c), Mihajlovic, Arsenijevic, Stefanovic, Djokic, Tirnanic, Marjanovic, Bek, Vujadinovic, Sekulic
Goals: Sekulic 4
Referee: Rego (Brazil)

Argentina and Uruguay qualified for final.

Stat Attack

The 1930 World Cup was the only one where a third-place play-off did not take place. Although some sources claim a match did occur (which Yugoslavia allegedly won 3-1), there is no real evidence to back this up. FIFA now recognises the USA as the third place team and Yugoslavia as the fourth, based on their overall record in the tournament.

World Cup Final

As expected, it was **Argentina** and **Uruguay**, the two teams who had played in the final of the Amsterdam Olympics football tournament in 1928, who would contest the first ever World Cup final. The hordes of home supporters crammed into the Centenario prayed for a repeat result. The Uruguayans, with Hector Castro returning to the starting line-up in place of the injured Anselmo, started unconvincingly but took the lead early in the game. It was young winger Pablo Dorado who would have the honour of scoring the first ever goal in a World Cup final, finishing off an impressive passing move by beating the hesitant Argentinean defence to a through-ball in the area, firing through the legs of goalkeeper Juan Botasso and in from the right side of the area. The stadium was filled with celebration but Argentina weren't about to sit back and let their great rivals claim the prize. They fought back strongly, the Uruguayans seemingly paralysed with nerves. Right winger Carlos Peucelle equalised midway through the half with a powerful shot and the Centenario was stunned when the prolific Guillermo Stabile outpaced Uruguay's defence to bundle in a right-wing cross for his eighth goal of the tournament and 2-1, a lead Argentina held to half-time. It was all going wrong for Uruguay but they came back after the break rejuvenated and set about getting themselves back in the game. Jose Nasazzi, their captain and inspiration, was everywhere and it was the right-back who created the hosts' equaliser just before the hour. He burst upfield from the back, running at the Argentine defence before squaring for Pedro Cea to blast home powerfully from the edge of the area. Back on level terms, Uruguay went for the throat and started to play some sumptuous football to outclass their opponents. They took the lead with twenty minutes remaining, outside left Santos Iriarte thundering home a spectacular goal to finish off a fine team move, unleashing a shot from range which flew past the bemused Botasso and into the top corner. Stabile hit the bar moments later but the chance was gone. The home crowd, realising their heroes were about to win the trophy they so desired, watched as the recalled Castro added a late fourth, heading in Dorado's cross to put some gloss on the scoreline. Uruguay were the first world champions and Nasazzi joyfully received the trophy from the man who had set the ball rolling in the first place: Jules Rimet.

> **Only at the World Cup**
>
> Argentina and Uruguay argued before the final because both wanted to use their own ball! In the end it was decided Argentina's would be used in the first half, Uruguay's in the second. Interestingly, both sides won the half they played with their ball!

> **Only at the World Cup**
>
> Few Argentinean supporters made it to cheer their team on in the final because of fog delaying the arrival of their boats! At least the ref was on an early one!

> **Only at the World Cup**
>
> Uruguay forward Hector Castro, scorer of his team's fourth goal in the final, had only one arm, accidentally amputating the other with a saw as a child! Luckily he was handier with a ball!

World Cup Final result

Uruguay 4-2 Argentina
30/07/30 – Montevideo (Centenario)
Uruguay: Ballesteros, Nasazzi (c), Mascheroni, Andrade, Fernandez, Gestido, Dorado, Scarone, Castro, Cea, Iriarte
Goals: Dorado 12, Cea 57, Iriarte 68, Castro 89
Argentina: Botasso, Della Torre, Paternoster, J Evaristo, Monti, Suarez, Peucelle, Varallo, Stabile, Ferreira (c), M Evaristo
Goals: Peucelle 20, Stabile 37
Referee: Langenus (Belgium)

Uruguay won the 1930 World Cup.

Tournament awards

Golden Boot: Guillermo Stabile (Argentina) – 8 goals
(Runner-up: Pedro Cea (Uruguay) – 5)

Best Player: Jose Nasazzi (Uruguay)

Best Goal: Santos Iriarte (Uruguay) – A rocket of a shot into the top corner from 25 yards after some fine build-up play in the final against Argentina.

Star XI:
Goalkeeper – Enrique Ballesteros (Uruguay)
Defenders – Jose Nasazzi (Uruguay), Milutin Ivkovic (Yugoslavia)
Midfielders – Jose Leandro Andrade (Uruguay), Luis Monti (Argentina), Alvaro Gestido (Uruguay)
Forwards – Hector Scarone (Uruguay), Guillermo Stabile (Argentina), Bert Patenaude (USA), Pedro Cea (Uruguay), Guillermo Subiabre (Chile)

World Cup Great – Jose Nasazzi (Uruguay)

Even in a country that has long been renowned for its attention to keeping things tight at the back and which has produced an astonishing array of world-class defenders over the years, Jose Nasazzi still shines brightly as Uruguay's greatest ever defender. 1950s legends Juan Schiaffino and Obdulio Varela may be considered by some to be better players but none could match the awesome Nasazzi for his vision and sweeping up at the back, qualities with which he was decades ahead of his time. Indeed, many Uruguayans still consider The Great Marshal to be their country's greatest ever player, despite the fact he plied his trade more than 80 years ago.

Starting out at Montevideo club Bella Vista, the young Nasazzi began to make a name for himself in the immediate aftermath of the First World War. His composed calm and leadership at the back were the scourge of many an attack and it wasn't long before he found himself at top side Nacional, the giants of the Uruguayan club game during the 1920s. He became part of a formidable line-up which won a series of domestic titles in the period. Nasazzi soon became a mainstay of the Uruguay side too and was named captain despite the fact he was only in his early 20s. At the age of 22 he led his country, including Nacional team mates Andres Mazali, Jose Leandro Andrade, Hector Scarone, Santos Urdinaran, Hector Castro and Pedro Cea among others, to victory in the 1923 Copa America. This was to be the start of a period of utter domination for Uruguay in international football.

Uruguay and Nasazzi first became renowned in Europe at the 1924 Olympics in Paris, when Nasazzi again captained the national team to the title, much to the Europeans' shock, as they considered their continent massively superior to the South Americans in footballing terms. Nasazzi and co proved this was no fluke by repeating the trick four years later in Amsterdam, where Argentina also proved the rise of South American football by being Uruguay's vanquished opponents in the final.

The national team's dominance was a key factor in FIFA's decision for the first ever World Cup to take place in Uruguay. The pressure therefore was firmly on the players, and on captain Nasazzi, then 29, in particular, to deliver the title. That they did was again testament to Nasazzi's skill at the back, which saw them concede just three goals in their four matches, and his inspirational leadership. It was Nasazzi who rallied his team mates to come back from 2-1 down against Argentina at half-time in the final and he was instrumental in the equaliser, bursting forward from the back to set up Cea for the goal. The match ended 4-2 and Nasazzi had the honour of being the first captain to receive the Jules Rimet Trophy, the feat for which he is most well known.

This would not be the end for Nasazzi but sadly he would never again have the chance to show his ability in a World Cup. Uruguay, hurt by the cream of European football boycotting their tournament in 1930, refused initially to attend World Cups hosted in the continent, denying Nasazzi and his all-conquering team the chance to defend their trophy in 1934, when they surely would have been formidable opponents even to Europe's best. His last hurrah would be in the 1935 Copa America, Nasazzi again leading Uruguay to victory, the fourth time he had won the trophy. He would retire at the age of 36 in 1937, boasting 51 caps, a hugely impressive record for the period.

Nasazzi was nominally a right-back but was much more akin in style to a modern-day sweeper. He frequently roamed behind his fellow defenders and half-backs, directing operations and clearing up danger where it developed before breaking forward when he gained possession rather than simply hoofing the ball up field like many defenders of the time. The sweeper position would not become a staple of international football until the late 1950s. That Nasazzi effectively invented the position almost 40 years earlier is just another string to the bow of one of the greatest defenders and captains of all time.

The first World Cup had been a huge success. The decision of Jules Rimet and the rest of FIFA to create it had been vindicated by a thrilling competition and there was no doubt that the World Cup had established itself as a fixture in the international calendar. The football had been high quality and the likes of the USA and Yugoslavia had been surprise packages, ensuring that there was at least some unpredictability in the tournament proceedings.

Uruguay, clearly the best side in the tournament, had deservedly carried off the trophy in front of their expectant home fans. The likes of Nasazzi, Andrade, Scarone, Cea and others had established themselves as bona fide international stars, the first World Cup heroes. There was no doubt that the best side had won the competition.

Argentina, meanwhile, had also been more than worthy of their place in the final. They and Uruguay were several notches above the other 11 sides in terms of ability and it showed, both teams comfortably winning all their games on route to the final. The Argentines too had seen stars emerge from their team, most notably midfield hardman Luis Monti and goal machine Guillermo Stabile, uncapped and unknown before the tournament but a World Cup legend after it. However, they had fallen at the final hurdle, beaten by a better team. Still, that was no consolation back home, where the furious fans rioted and protested for months, culminating in a violent military coup and the deposing of the country's president!

The European teams who had made the trip, meanwhile, had done considerably better than many had feared. Yugoslavia had been the pick of them, deservedly beating Brazil and reaching the semi-finals before being battered by the hosts. France and Romania too had shone in patches, both gaining an impressive and well-earned victory in their groups before losing to the eventual finalists. Only Belgium had performed below expectations.

Nevertheless, there was no doubt that with the withdrawal of all Europe's best teams, the field had been weakened significantly. As a result, the tournament was considerably less competitive than it might have been, illustrated by the ease with which Argentina and Uruguay advanced to the final. Europe's boycott of the tournament also understandably infuriated the Uruguayans and sadly would lead to this great side's absence from the next two World Cups.

1934: Italy

Qualification

32 Entrants.

Group 1

Sweden 6-2 Estonia, Lithuania 0-2 Sweden, Estonia v Lithuania cancelled as neither side could qualify

	Pld	W	D	L	GF	GA	Pts
Sweden	2	2	0	0	8	2	4
Lithuania	1	0	0	1	0	2	0
Estonia	1	0	0	1	2	6	0

Sweden qualified

Group 2

Spain 9-0 Portugal, Portugal 1-2 Spain

	Pld	W	D	L	GF	GA	Pts
Spain	2	2	0	0	11	1	4
Portugal	2	0	0	2	1	11	0

Spain qualified

Group 3

Italy 4-0 Greece, Greece withdrew before return leg

Italy qualified

Stat Attack

The 1934 World Cup was the only occasion where the hosts were forced to qualify. Thankfully, they managed it with an easy win over Greece.

Group 4

Bulgaria 1-4 Hungary, Austria 6-1 Bulgaria, Hungary 4-1 Bulgaria
Bulgaria withdrew; Austria and Hungary did not play each other as they were already assured of qualification.

Hungary and **Austria** qualified.

Group 5

Poland 1-2 Czechoslovakia, Poland withdrew before return leg

Czechoslovakia qualified.

Group 6

Yugoslavia 2-2 Switzerland, Switzerland 2-2 Romania (Romania fielded an ineligible player, FIFA awarded Switzerland a 2-0 win), Romania 2-1 Yugoslavia

	Pld	W	D	L	GF	GA	Pts
Switzerland	2	1	1	0	4	2	3
Romania	2	1	0	1	2	3	2
Yugoslavia	2	0	1	1	3	4	1

Switzerland and **Romania** qualified.

Group 7

Ireland 4-4 Belgium, Holland 5-2 Ireland, Belgium 2-4 Holland

	Pld	W	D	L	GF	GA	Pts
Holland	2	2	0	0	9	4	4
Belgium	2	0	1	1	6	8	1
Ireland	2	0	1	1	6	9	1

Holland and **Belgium** qualified.

Group 8

Luxembourg 1-9 Germany, Luxembourg 1-6 France, Germany v France cancelled because both teams had already qualified.

	Pld	W	D	L	GF	GA	Pts
Germany	1	1	0	0	9	1	2
France	1	1	0	0	6	1	2
Luxembourg	2	0	0	2	2	15	0

Germany and **France** qualified.

Group 9

Peru withdrew.

Brazil qualified.

Group 10

Chile withdrew.

Argentina qualified.

Group 11

Haiti v Cuba (in Haiti): 1-3, 1-1, 0-6 (agg. 2-10)
Mexico v Cuba (in Mexico): 3-2, 5-0, 4-1 (agg. 12-3)
USA v Mexico (in Italy): 4-2

USA qualified.

Group 12

Turkey withdrew.
Egypt 7-1 Palestine, Palestine 1-4 Egypt

	Pld	W	D	L	GF	GA	Pts
Egypt	2	2	0	0	11	2	4
Palestine	2	0	0	2	2	11	0

Egypt qualified.

Stat Attack

Uruguay became the only World Cup holders not to defend their title in the finals after they decided to boycott the 1934 tournament as a mark of revenge against the many European teams, including Italy, who had not attended the 1930 competition in their own country.

The Contenders

Argentina
Austria
Belgium
Brazil
Czechoslovakia
Egypt
France
Germany
Holland
Hungary
Italy
Romania
Spain
Sweden
Switzerland
USA

The Italy of Benito Mussolini won the right to be the first European country to host the World Cup, persuading Sweden, who had also bid initially, to withdraw in favour of them. It was the chance Italy's fascist government had wanted to try to paint a rose-tinted portrait of their country to the outside world. Mussolini and his henchmen would be in attendance to watch their national side do battle against the world's best teams and they would not take kindly to defeat.

Just as the debut World Cup in South American had been dominated by South American sides, the 1934 World Cup was packed with European teams, who made up 12 of the 16 sides present after qualification, including all the favourites. There looked little prospect of a team from outside Europe carrying off the trophy, especially as reigning champions Uruguay, still angry with the mass withdrawal of Europe's best teams from the tournament they hosted four years previously, had understandably decided they would not take part. Everything looked set for the Europeans to re-establish their dominance of the international game.

FIFA had abandoned the group format used in 1930 and instead implemented a straight knockout system, meaning that eight of the 16 finalists would play just one game in the tournament before being forced to return home, in some cases thousands of miles and weeks of travel away. This was a journey poor Mexico had already been forced to make, as a late entry by the USA had forced the Central Americans to play their neighbours to the north in Rome three days before the start of the tournament. Mexico had lost 4-2 and were out of the tournament before it had even started. The Americans, meanwhile, joined the other 15 teams in the finals.

With a fine side and home advantage, Vittorio Pozzo's **Italy** were widely regarded as favourites for the tournament. With Mussolini there to watch them perform the fascist salute before matches, there would be huge pressure on them from "Il Duce" to succeed but the quality of the players at their disposal looked to be able to offset this, in particular brilliant Inter Milan inside forward Giuseppe Meazza. They would also, controversially, have four Argentineans in their squad: Luis Monti, Attilio Demaria (both of whom had played in Argentina's run to the 1930 World Cup final), Raimundo Orsi and Enrique Guaita. The use of these "oriundi" was justified by Pozzo with his claims that their Italian ancestry would have made them eligible for national service in the First World War, stating: "If they can die for Italy, they can also play for Italy." The Italians could also call upon Pozzo's tactical adaptation of the standard and widely employed 2-3-5 pyramid formation, with his Metodo system seeing the inside forwards drop deeper, operating in what we would call "the hole" today, to help link the play. They would be the team to beat in the tournament.

They would certainly be challenged, however, by **Austria**, the "Wunderteam", who coach Hugo Meisl had turned into the most feared side in Europe. It was their attack that made the best reading, deep-lying centre forward Matthias Sindelar their elegant playmaker and the prolific youngster Josef Bican, who would go on to score more goals in competitive matches in his career than any other player in history, their deadly cutting edge. They would most likely be the main challengers to the hosts. Austria's neighbours **Hungary** were another fancied side. Big centre forward Gyorgy Sarosi, who could also play centre half if needed, headed up a strong side who had long been one of the best teams in the world, even if they were now shorn of some of the cutting edge of the side inspired by Imre Schlosser-Lakatos and co which had been so impressive in the previous two decades.

Spain were another highly regarded European side. With legendary goalkeeper Ricardo Zamora, without a doubt the greatest custodian of the pre-Second World War period, between the sticks, they would be tough to beat, giving their forwards space with which to work. **Czechoslovakia** too came with a chance. They had their own star goalkeeper, Frantisek Planicka, who lost very little in comparison even to Zamora. Allied to this was a formidable forward line, including the dangerous Oldrich Nejedly and the speedy Antonin Puc. **Germany** could not be ruled out either. Powerful 19-year-old forward Edmund Conen looked like a dangerous prospect for an improving team, while Fritz Szepan and Paul Janes would roam behind.

Three of the four European sides who had competed in 1930 had returned, with only Yugoslavia missing out. None of them were among the favourites, however. **France**, the World Cup's creators, seemed to have little hope of winning their trophy. Several of their 1930 squad would return, including history-maker Lucien Laurent, goalkeeper Alex Thepot and schemer Edmond Delfour, but there looked little prospect of them making a mark on the tournament, especially as they had been drawn to play mighty Austria. Their neighbours **Belgium** would also likely struggle in their clash with Germany. Forwards Bernard Voorhoof and Louis Versijp returned but there was little hope of an improved performance. **Romania**, who had qualified ahead of the Yugoslavs, looked probably the best of the three but even the good work of Emerich Vogl and Nicolae Covaci would likely not be enough.

Europe's final three representative, **Sweden**, **Switzerland** and **Holland**, would be among those making their tournament debuts. All came with some hope of progress but were not serious candidates for the title. However, they would be desperate to make their presence felt and secure progress at least to the quarter-finals.

Argentina had been impressive finalists four years earlier but a repeat in Italy looked incredibly unlikely. With their best players drafted into the ranks of the hosts, they deliberately left their remaining stars at home, so as to avoid Italian clubs poaching them too. The inexperienced players they did bring would be unlikely to be able to compete with the Europeans. There was a similar story with **Brazil**, who were also missing several of their domestic stars. At least in 20-year-old striker Leonidas they had a potential star player capable of turning a game in an instant. The **USA**, the 1930 tournament's surprise package, looked unlikely to repeat their success this time round. They had retained just a handful of their stars of four years previous and would have only three days to prepare for the competition after their last-minute qualifying tie against Mexico. The final qualifiers were **Egypt**, Africa's first representative and the biggest outsiders of all. Their biggest claim to fame was their victory over Hungary in the 1924 Olympics. Intriguingly they would face the same opponents again in the first round, the Hungarians unlikely to take them as lightly this time round.

> **Stat Attack**
>
> Egypt were the first ever African side to compete in the final stages of the World Cup.

Debutants: Austria, Czechoslovakia, Egypt, Germany, Holland, Hungary, Italy, Spain, Sweden, Switzerland

The Draw

Italy v USA
Brazil v Spain
Egypt v Hungary
Austria v France
Czechoslovakia v Romania
Holland v Switzerland
Argentina v Sweden
Belgium v Germany

Venues:
Rome, Bologna, Florence, Genoa, Milan, Naples, Trieste, Turin

The Tournament – 27 May-10 June

First Round

All eight of the first-round games were played simultaneously across the country in the eight stadia set aside for the tournament. Kicking things off in the Stadium of the National Fascist Party in Rome were hosts **Italy**, who took on the **USA** in front of the watchful eyes of Mussolini. To the dictator's delight, the match proved the simplest of victories for the Italians. The US were a shadow of the side who had caused such a stir four years earlier and fell apart in the wake of the Italians' relentless attacks. Despite their dominance, it took Italy almost 20 minutes to open their account. However, when they did finally find the way to goal, the flood gates opened, Angelo Schiavio and Raimundo Orsi both scoring in the space of a couple of minutes. Schiavio added a third on the half hour and the hosts went into the break in complete control. The US briefly threatened a comeback in the second half when Aldo Donelli pulled one back but alas for them the goals were to arrive at the other end. Giovanni Ferrari restored Italy's three-goal cushion and Schiavio completed his hat-trick a minute later, Orsi doubling his tally soon after. The brilliant Giuseppe Meazza, a thorn in the Americans' side all afternoon, added goal number seven late on. The battered Americans limped back across the Atlantic licking their wounds. For Mussolini's Italy, it had been the perfect start.

> **Only at the World Cup**
>
> On the orders of their fascist government, the Italian team performed the straight-arm fascist salute before all their games in the 1934 World Cup.

> **Stat Attack**
>
> Italy's 7-1 trouncing of the USA is both Italy's biggest ever World Cup win and the USA's biggest ever World Cup defeat.

Meanwhile in Genoa, **Brazil** were proven a limited team by a fine **Spain** outfit, who were well deserving of their 3-1 win. They were much quicker out of the blocks than the lethargic South

Americans, taking the lead through a penalty from Jose Iraragorri. The forward soon doubled his tally before young striker Isidro Langara killed the game with a third, and all in the space of just half an hour's play. If the Spanish thought the game was won at half-time, however, they were mistaken. Brazil were much improved after the break, Leonidas deservedly pulling a goal back with ten minutes played. Indeed, if Waldemar had converted a penalty seven minutes later instead of seeing Ricardo Zamora pull off a fine save it might have been a different story. As it was, Zamora and his defensive colleagues held out to eliminate the Brazilians, who had again come up just short against superior opponents, as they had in their defeat to the Yugoslavs in 1930. Spain had proven they were a dangerous side and would go into the quarter-finals full of confidence.

Hungary looked to lay the ghosts of the 1924 Olympics in their clash with **Egypt** in Naples. They started well enough and soon had a two-goal lead, forwards Pal Teleki and Geza Toldi on target early in the first half. However, as in Paris ten years earlier, the Egyptians showed no respect for their supposedly superior opponents, giving them no time on the ball and hassling them continually. They were to get their reward when inside forward Abdel Fawzi scored twice to see them incredibly go in level at half-time and they could dream of another unlikely win over the European heavyweights. However, it was not to be, as Fawzi had a third controversially disallowed and Hungary recovered from their shaky patch in the second half to win comfortably in the end, dangerous inside right Jeno Vincze putting them back in front and Toldi, despite a clear foul on keeper Mustafa Mansour, grabbing his second for a final score of 4-2. The Africans could hold their heads up high and they had played their part in an enthralling contest but it was Hungary who would be going through, no doubt helped by the performance of the referee.

> **Only at the World Cup**
>
> The performance of Italian referee Barlassina no doubt helped Hungary win against Egypt. Fawzi scored a fine third goal but it was dubiously disallowed for offside before Toldi's fourth for Hungary was gained by fouling the keeper but still stood.

In Turin, the Wunderteam of **Austria** opened their tournament against **France**. It was expected to be a fairly gentle opener for the much-fancied Austrians but they made remarkably heavy weather of disposing of their limited opponents. Hugo Meisl's side were slow at the start, seemingly drifting along in second gear. Centre forward Jean Nicolas awoke them from their lethargy, opening the scoring after 18 minutes to put the French into a shock lead. They held this advantage until the very end of the half, Matthias Sindelar finally showing what he could do with a well-taken equaliser. However, the Austrians still were unable to find their form, even after an injury to Nicolas caused the French to battle on with just ten men, and the game drifted into extra time. Finally, Austria remembered why they were such a feared side, strikers Anton Schall and Josef Bican securing the win, though there was a hint of offside in the first goal. The French did grab another consolation goal late on, Georges Verriest firing in from the spot, but it was not enough to keep their tournament alive. Austria had scraped through to the quarter-finals by the skin of their teeth. Surely, they would not be so bad again.

Trieste saw Eastern European sides **Czechoslovakia** and **Romania** do battle. The Czechs were largely favoured but no-one had told Romania, who took an early lead through Stefan Dobai. It looked as if the Czechs would be heading home early from the tournament until Antonin Puc and Oldrich Nejedly rescued their side with crucial second-half goals. Still, the Romanians continued to press and could well have taken the game into extra time or even won it had it not been for the brilliance of Frantisek Planicka in the Czech goal, whose heroics denied Romania on several occasions. As in 1930, the Romanians would be heading home after the first round.

At Milan's San Siro stadium, European debutants **Holland** and **Switzerland** locked horns. Most expected the Swiss to win and so it proved, though few would have predicted the Dutch to run them as close as they did. It all looked to be going according to plan when Leopold Kielholz put the Swiss ahead after seven minutes. However, they had reckoned without the Dutch resolve, which saw Kick Smit equalise soon after. Try as they might, however, the Swiss were the better side and made it count either side of half-time, Kielholz adding his second before Andre Abegglen gave Switzerland the two-goal cushion they so desired. Still, Leen Vente's late goal kept the Swiss sweating right to the finish and they had been made to work much harder for their win than most had predicted. The Dutch would return home with pride firmly intact.

While this was happening, **Argentina** were seeking to call upon the spirit of 1930 to overcome **Sweden** in Bologna. However, this proved too much for their inexperienced side and they went out at the first hurdle. Nevertheless, they certainly put up a fight and were far from disgraced, making the Scandinavians work extremely hard for their victory. The Argentineans took a surprise lead after just four minutes, defender Ernesto Belis scoring directly from a free-kick. The Swedes, forced to chase the game, responded in kind, prolific centre forward Sven Jonasson equalising five minutes later and the score remained 1-1 until just after the break. If Sweden thought the danger was gone after their equaliser, they were proved wrong when the South Americans regained the lead just after half-time, inside forward Alberto Galateo on target to restore their advantage. That was as good as it got for Argentina, however, as the Swedes started to put their best football together to outclass their weakened opponents, Jonasson scoring his second to level things up again before Knut Kroon got the winner ten minutes from the end. Sweden had proven they had the strength of character to battle to victory and had shown themselves capable of playing some good football. Argentina, meanwhile, were beaten but far from humiliated.

> **Only at the World Cup**
>
> Argentina deliberately took a weakened squad to Italy to avoid the Europeans poaching their best players, as Pozzo's Italy had already done. Given the side they took consisted of inexperienced amateurs, they could be proud of their narrow 3-2 defeat to Sweden.

Elsewhere, **Germany** and **Belgium** clashed in Florence. Stanislaus Kobierski put Germany in front midway through the first period but they fatally relaxed immediately afterwards and were promptly punished by the ever-alert Bernard Voorhoof, who helped himself to a brace to put the Belgians 2-1 up at half-time. However, the Germans came out a different side after the break and captain Fritz Szepan began increasingly to run the show. Otto Siffling equalised four minutes after the break before young striker Edmund Conen took centre stage, outmuscling the Belgian defence and helping himself to a 21-minute hat-trick. Finishing 5-2, the Germans had eventually shown what they could do and had been too strong for the brave Belgians.

First Round results

Italy 7-1 USA
27/05/34 – Rome (Stadio Nazionale PNF)
Italy: Combi, Rosetta (c), Allemandi, Pizziolo, Monti, Bertolini, Guarisi, Meazza, Schiavio, Ferrari, Orsi
Goals: Schiavio 18, 29, 64, Orsi 20, 69, Ferrari 63, Meazza 90
USA: Hjulian, Czerkiewicz, Moorhouse (c), Pietras, Gonsalves, Florie, Ryan, Nilsen, Donelli, Dick, McLean
Goals: Donelli 57
Referee: Mercet (Switzerland)

Brazil 1-3 Spain
27/05/34 – Genoa (Luigi Ferraris)
Brazil: Pedrosa, Sylvio, Luz, Tinoco, Martim Silveira (c), Canalli, Luizinho, Waldemar, Leonidas, Armandinho, Patesko
Goals: Leonidas 55
Spain: Zamora (c), Ciriaco, Quincoces, Cilaurren, Muguerza, Marculeta, Iraragorri, Langara, Lecue, Lafuente, Gorostiza
Goals: Iraragorri pen 18, 25, Langara 29
Referee: Birlem (Germany)

Egypt 2-4 Hungary
27/05/34 – Naples (Giorgio Ascarelli)
Egypt: Mansour, Ali Shafi, Hamidu, El Far, Rafaat, Raghab, Latif, Fawzi, Moukhtar (c), Taha, Hassan
Goals: Fawzi 31, 39
Hungary: A Szabo, Futo, Sternberg (c), Palotas, Szucs, Lazar, Markos, Vincze, Teleki, Toldi, G Szabo
Goals: Teleki 11, Toldi 27, 61, Vincze 53
Referee: Barlassina (Italy)

Austria 3-2 France (aet)
27/05/34 – Turin (Benito Mussolini)
Austria: Platzer, Cisar, Sesta, Wagner, Smistik (c), Urbanek, Zischek, Bican, Sindelar, Schall, Viertl
Goals: Sindelar 44, Schall 93, Bican 109
France: Thepot, Mairesse, Mattler, Delfour, Verriest (c), Lietaer, Keller, Alcazar, Nicolas, Rio, Aston
Goals: Nicolas 18, Verriest pen 116
Referee: Van Moorsel (Holland)

Czechoslovakia 2-1 Romania
27/05/34 – Trieste (Littorio)
Czechoslovakia: Planicka (c), Zenisek, Ctyroky, Kostalek, Cambal, Krcil, Junek, Silny, Sobotka, Nejedly, Puc
Goals: Puc 50, Nejedly 67
Romania: Zombori, Vogl (c), Albu, Deheleanu, Cotormani, Moravet, Bindea, Covaci, Sepi, Bodola, Dobai
Goals: Dobai 11
Referee: Langenus (Belgium)

Holland 2-3 Switzerland
27/05/34 – Milan (San Siro)
Holland: Van der Meulen, Weber, Van Run, Pellikaan, Anderiesen, Van Heel (c), Wels, Vente, Bakhuys, Smit, Van Nellen
Goals: Smit 19, Vente 84
Switzerland: Sechehaye, Minelli (c), W Weiler, Guinchard, Jaccard, Hufschmid, Von Kanel, Passello, Kielholz, Abegglen, Bossi
Goals: Kielholz 7, 43, Abegglen 69
Referee: Eklind (Sweden)

Argentina 2-3 Sweden
27/05/34 – Bologna (Littoriale)
Argentina: Freschi, Pedevilla, Belis, Nehin, Urbieta Sosa, Lopez (c), Rua, Wilde, De Vincenzi, Galateo, Iraneta
Goals: Belis 4, Galateo 48
Sweden: Rydberg, Axelsson, S Andersson, Carlsson, Rosen (c), E Andersson, Dunker, Gustavsson, Jonasson, Keller, Kroon
Goals: Jonasson 9, 67, Kroon 79
Referee: Braun (Austria)

Belgium 2-5 Germany
27/05/34 – Florence (Giovanni Berta)
Belgium: Van de Weyer, Smellinckx, Joacim, Peeraer, Welkenhuysen (c), Claessens, Devries, Voorhoof, Capelle, Grimmonprez, Heremans
Goals: Voorhoof 29, 43
Germany: Kress, Haringer, Schwartz, Janes, Szepan (c), Zielinski, Lehner, Hohmann, Conen, Siffling, Kobierski
Goals: Kobierski 25, Siffling 49, Conen 66, 70, 87
Referee: Mattea (Italy)

Italy, Spain, Hungary, Austria, Czechoslovakia, Switzerland, Sweden and Germany qualified for quarter-finals.

Quarter-finals

As with the first-round matches, all four of the quarter-finals were played simultaneously. Two of the most impressive performers in their opening games, **Italy** and **Spain**, faced each other in Florence. The Italians were generally favoured but the Spanish roared out of the blocks and took a deserved lead half an hour in as Luis Regueiro beat Giampiero Combi in the Italy goal. Behind, the Italians laid siege to the Spanish goal but were denied time and time again by the heroic Zamora. It was to take a shocking refereeing decision to let the Italians back into the game, Zamora clearly fouled as Giovanni Ferrari stabbed in from close range but referee Baert somehow let the goal stand. Still, there would be no further goals in the game, as the two sides resorted instead to fouling each other repeatedly. Extra time came and went and a replay would be needed to separate the teams.

> **Stat Attack**
>
> Amazingly, Italy and Spain's 1-1 stalemate was the first ever World Cup draw, in its 27th game!

Elsewhere, tempers were to flare in Bologna also, as neighbours **Austria** and **Hungary** did battle. Both these heavyweights of world football were renowned for their skilful attacking play but sadly it was their darker sides that were more in evidence in this brutal clash. Johann Horvath, in at the expense of Anton Schall up front for the Austrians, put his side ahead early on and Karl Zischek doubled the advantage after the break. Gyorgy Sarosi briefly gave his side hope with a penalty on the hour but the final 30 minutes of the game simply degenerated into what Austria coach Hugo Meisl described as a "brawl." Both teams took to fouling each other with relish, leaving several players writhing on the floor in agony. The most brutal of these challenges proved sufficient for Hungary's Imre Markos to receive his marching orders as the frustration of impending elimination boiled over into violence. The Wunderteam were into the semi-finals without ever being forced into playing their best football. Their campaign seemed to be gaining momentum and they would be formidable opposition for any team.

> **Stat Attack**
>
> Hungary's Imre Markos was the only player sent off in the 1934 World Cup.

Meanwhile, a far more enticing game was taking place in Turin, where **Switzerland** and **Czechoslovakia** served up a feast of attacking football. The prolific Kielholz was again on target to put the Swiss ahead early on but this proved only the cue for the Czechs to start playing their best football. Frantisek Svoboda, a new addition to the starting line-up, equalised barely five minutes later and Jiri Sobotka pounced just after half-time to leave Czechoslovakia firmly in the driving seat. However, there was to be a final flurry of action at the death, Willy Jaggi looking to have earned the Swiss the right to take the game into extra time with a late leveller before Oldrich Nejedly broke their hearts moments later, firing home in the dying seconds to take the Czechs through. Czechoslovakia had again shown they could compete with the tournament's best, while the Swiss had demonstrated they could play good football but had ultimately come up short.

In Milan, **Germany** also booked their ticket to the last four against **Sweden**, though they were no doubt helped by the Swedes suffering an early injury which forced them to fight on with a man down. Nevertheless, they bravely held out until a quick-fire double from forward Karl Hohmann just past the hour sunk them. That surely was that but the heroic Scandinavians were not about to give up. Gosta Dunker caused the Germans in the crowd to spend a tense final ten minutes when he pulled a goal back but ultimately an equaliser remained beyond them. Germany had done just enough and would carry their impressive campaign on into the semi-finals.

> **Only at the World Cup**
>
> The performance of Swiss referee Rene Mercet in Italy's replay with Spain was shockingly biased towards the home side, including ignoring a foul on Spain's keeper for the only goal and disallowing two perfectly good Spanish goals! The Swiss FA, ashamed by his performance, dropped him from the roster on his return to the country. One Swiss paper wrote: "Mercet favoured the Italians in a most shameful manner." Allegations would later emerge that Mussolini's officials had bribed several referees so that they would favour Italy. There's nothing like accepting bribes from a fascist dictator to make your popularity fall!

Less than 24 hours after the end of their quarter-final clash, the exhausted members of the **Italy** and **Spain** teams were forced to galvanise themselves for a **replay**. Both sides were forced into changes to rest tired bodies, with the most notable casualty being Spain's captain and star keeper Ricardo Zamora. This was to prove crucial, as his replacement, Juan Jose Nogues, was not in the same class as Spain's number one. Still, Italy's winning goal, a header from Meazza 11 minutes in, should have been disallowed for a foul on the keeper. The Italians, though, got their goal and the benefit of the doubt in several other dubious decisions as referee Mercet seemed to side with the home crowd, disallowing what seemed like two perfectly good Spanish goals. Spain were furious at the end but they had lost, robbed by the scandalous performance of the referee.

Quarter-final results

Italy 1-1 Spain (aet)
31/05/34 – Florence (Giovanni Berta)
Italy: Combi (c), Monzeglio, Allemandi, Pizziolo, Monti, Castellazzi, Guaita, Meazza, Schiavio, Ferrari, Orsi
Goals: Ferrari 44
Spain: Zamora (c), Ciriaco, Quincoces, Cillauren, Muguerza, Lafuente, Iraragorri, Langara, Fede, Regueiro, Gorostiza
Goals: Regueiro 30
Referee: Baert (Belgium)

Hungary 1-2 Austria
31/05/34 – Bologna (Littoriale)
Hungary: A Szabo, Vago, Sternberg (c), Palotas, Szucs, Szalay, Markos, Avar, Sarosi, Toldi, Kemeny
Goals: Sarosi pen 60
Sent off: Markos 63
Austria: Platzer, Cisar, Sesta, Wagner, Smistik (c), Urbanek, Zischek, Bican, Sindelar, Horvath, Viertl
Goals: Horvath 8, Zischek 51
Referee: Mattea (Italy)

Czechoslovakia 3-2 Switzerland
31/05/34 – Turin (Benito Mussolini)
Czechoslovakia: Planicka (c), Zenisek, Ctyroky, Kostalek, Cambal, Krcil, Junek, Svoboda, Sobotka, Nejedly, Puc
Goals: Svoboda 24, Sobotka 49, Nejedly 82
Switzerland: Sechehaye, Minelli (c), W Weiler, Guinchard, Jaccard, Hufschmid, Von Kanel, Jaggi, Kielholz, Abegglen, Jack
Goals: Kielholz 18, Jaggi 78
Referee: Beranek (Austria)

Sweden 1-2 Germany
31/05/34 – Milan (San Siro)
Sweden: Rydberg, Axelsson, S Andersson, Carlsson, Rosen (c), E Andersson, Dunker, Gustavsson, Jonasson, Keller, Kroon
Goals: Dunker 82
Germany: Kress, Haringer, Busch, Gramlich, Szepan (c), Zielinski, Lehner, Hohmann, Conen, Siffling, Kobierski
Goals: Hohmann 60, 63
Referee: Barlassina (Italy)

Replay

Italy 1-0 Spain
01/06/34 – Florence (Giovanni Berta)
Italy: Combi (c), Monzeglio, Allemandi, Ferraris, Monti, Bertolini, Guaita, Meazza, Borel, Demaria, Orsi
Goals: Meazza 11
Spain: Nogues, Zabalo, Quincoces (c), Cillauren, Muguerza, Lecue, Ventolra, Regueiro, Campanal, Chacho, Bosch
Referee: Mercet (Switzerland)

Italy, Austria, Czechoslovakia and Germany qualified for semi-finals.

Semi-finals

Italy had emerged victorious from their controversial clash with Spain but a semi-final win seemed a long shot, since not only would the exhausted team have only two days to recover from the gruelling replay but their opponents in Milan would be the Wunderteam of **Austria**. However, coach Vittorio Pozzo managed to motivate his shattered players to produce a fantastic performance which caught the complacent Austrians cold. As the rain lashed down on the San Siro, the Austrians stuck to their neat, attacking football but struggled to create their usual rhythm in the atrocious weather. They were punished when Argentine-born winger Enrique Guaita put the Italians in front early on and it could have been more, the home side producing a fine performance. Eventually, Austria did remember how to play football and launched a last-ditch assault on the Italian goal. However, Italy's midfield trio of Attilio Ferraris, Luis Monti and Luigi Bertolini excelled and captain Giampiero Combi stood firm between the sticks, producing a string of fine saves to deny his desperate opponents. In the end they had done enough, deservedly beating the giants of the European game against all odds. Austria, desperately disappointed, had again been victims of their own complacency. The third-place play-off and not the final would be their next port of call.

At the same time in Rome, **Czechoslovakia** and **Germany** met to decide who would be the hosts' opponents in the final. The Czechs, impressive throughout the tournament, were far the superior side

> **Only at the World Cup**
>
> Germany's equaliser in their defeat to Czechoslovakia came from a costly misjudgement from goalkeeper Planicka. Noack shot from range, the keeper, expecting it to drift wide, didn't react but the ball flew past him into the back of the net! Whoops!

throughout the game and eventually made their dominance count with a 3-1 win. It was not all plain sailing but the Czechs started strongly, deservedly taking an early lead when a shot from Frantisek Junek was deflected into the path of the lurking Oldrich Nejedly, who fired it home gratefully. The Czechs' high-tempo, attacking football had Germany chasing shadows and they should have gone on to dominate the game but a rare mistake from goalkeeper and captain Frantisek Planicka gifted the Germans an equaliser, the big custodian failing to react to Rudolf Noack's shot from range which flew into the back of the net. The Czechs were to make their evident superiority count, however, Nejedly scoring twice more late on to complete his hat-trick and take Czechoslovakia into the final. There was no doubt that the dangerous Czechs were worthy of their place.

Semi-final results

Italy 1-0 Austria
03/06/34 – Milan (San Siro)
Italy: Combi (c), Monzeglio, Allemandi, Ferraris, Monti, Bertolini, Guaita, Meazza, Schiavio, Ferrari, Orsi
Goals: Guaita 19
Austria: Platzer, Cisar, Sesta, Wagner, Smistik (c), Urbanek, Zischek, Bican, Sindelar, Schall, Viertl
Referee: Eklind (Sweden)

Czechoslovakia 3-1 Germany
03/06/34 – Rome (Stadio Nazionale PNF)
Czechoslovakia: Planicka (c), Burgr, Ctyroky, Kostalek, Cambal, Krcil, Junek, Svoboda, Sobotka, Nejedly, Puc
Goals: Nejedly 21, 69, 80
Germany: Kress, Haringer, Busch, Bender, Szepan (c), Zielinski, Lehner, Noack, Conen, Siffling, Kobierski
Goals: Noack 62
Referee: Barlassina (Italy)

Italy and Czechoslovakia qualified for final, Austria and Germany to third-place play-off.

World Cup Great – Matthias Sindelar (Austria)

For the large part of the 1920s and early 30s, Austria were unopposed as the best side in Europe. The "Wunderteam", with maverick manager Hugo Meisl at the helm, were all but unstoppable. They boasted some fine players during that period, including reliable keeper Rudi Hiden, dominant centre half and captain Josef Smistik and later on prolific strikers Josef Bican, Anton Schall and Franz Binder. Of all the side's players, though, none could hold a candle to the talents of their figurehead and inspiration, the brilliant centre forward Matthias Sindelar.

Born in the modern day Czech Republic at a time when it was still part of the Austro-Hungarian Empire, Sindelar's family moved to Vienna when he was still a baby and it was in the youth ranks of Hertha Vienna that the youngster first started to make his name. Tall, sinewy but with a fantastic touch and unrivalled vision, Sindelar was blessed with footballing ability that most could only dream of. Signing for the club that would soon become Austria Wien, the young Sindelar instantly established himself as his team's creative hub and the honours started racking up, winning one Austrian title and five domestic cups in his time at the club, where he would spend the rest of his career.

Appropriately, the 23-year-old forward made his international debut against the country of his birth, Czechoslovakia, scoring in a 2-1 victory. From then on, Sindelar never looked back, establishing himself as the key player in an outstanding side. He would play for Austria a total of 43 times in his career, scoring an impressive 27 goals and setting up countless more for his team mates.

Sindelar's only World Cup appearance came in 1934 when exciting young striker Bican was just beginning to emerge on the international scene. The calm experience and subtle promptings of Sindelar proved the perfect counterpart for the youngster's goalscoring prowess and so it was little surprise that Austria were many people's favourites to win the tournament. It was not to be, however. The Austrians were oddly lethargic in scraping by France in the first round, though Sindelar was excellent in dictating the play, scoring a deserved goal. The veteran then ran the show brilliantly against Hungary in an impressive quarter-final victory before it all came to an end on a sodden pitch in the semi-finals, where they went out to hosts Italy amid some dubious refereeing.

Sindelar and Austria qualified again for the 1938 tournament but the country was annexed by Hitler's Germany shortly before the competition and Austria were forced to withdraw, their best players stolen by the Germans. Sindelar, however, who was not shy in his contempt of the Nazis, twice defied them with astonishing bravery. First, in Austria's last international, a propaganda-driven clash with Germany, he defied team orders, since the sides had been told to play out a diplomatic draw, scoring the first and proving the catalyst for a 2-0 victory, openly challenging the Nazis. Then, Sindelar refused to play for Germany, despite the fact he was the player Hitler's government most wanted in their team, using injury and his increasing age as excuses to stand up to the Nazis again.

This was a dangerous game that Sindelar was playing, however, and it ended in tragedy in January 1939, when he and his girlfriend were found dead in their flat from carbon monoxide poisoning. The official verdict was accidental death but it was widely believed that the pair either committed suicide or were murdered by the Nazis. They had paid the ultimate price for Sindelar's courage in the face of tyranny.

Despite being listed as a centre forward, Sindelar actually was one of the first midfield generals along with Italy's Giuseppe Meazza. Sindelar would drop back behind his fellow forwards to find more space and from there he could dictate the play, as he did so impressively time and again for Austria. It was a strategy that Nandor Hidegkuti would use famously 20 years later for Hungary but Sindelar had sown the seeds two decades earlier. A genius on the field and an idealist off it, Matthias Sindelar remains to this day Austria's best and most respected footballer of all time.

Third-place Play-off

In Naples, semi-final losers **Austria** and **Germany** were forced to overcome their disappointment and play for the bronze medal, the first time there had been a match for third place incorporated into the World Cup format. The value of such a game between two disappointed teams remains questionable to this day but it has been present ever since. Most of these games have seen one team care much more about finishing third than the other and this was no exception. In this case, Austria, on paper one of the best two sides in the tournament, were clearly devastated by their defeat to Italy four days earlier. With star man Matthias Sindelar rested, they cared little about the game. Germany, in contrast, were eager to win and claim the third place which would mean so much to their developing football nation. This greater passion told as early as the very first minute, when Ernst Lehner put the Germans ahead. Playing with a desire absent from the largely disinterested Austrians, Germany scored a second through Edmund Conen before Johann Horvath did manage to put Austria on the scoresheet. Nevertheless, Lehner had his second before half-time and though defender Karl Sesta did pull one back in the second half, the Germans claimed the victory they desired. However, on the rare occasions the Austrians did start to play football, they easily embarrassed the Germans with their movement and passing. Still, Germany's third place was a terrific achievement, while for Austria, their first World Cup had ended up being something of a disappointment for a side who had built up such a fearsome reputation for themselves in the previous decade.

Third-place Play-off result

Austria 2-3 Germany
07/06/34 – Naples (Giorgio Ascarelli)
Austria: Platzer, Cisar, Sesta, Wagner, Smistik (c), Urbanek, Zischek, Bican, Braun, Horvath, Viertl
Goals: Horvath 28, Sesta 54
Germany: Jakob, Janes, Busch, Munzenberg, Szepan (c), Zielinski, Bender, Lehner, Conen, Siffling, Heidemann
Goals: Lehner 1, 42, Conen 27
Referee: Carraro (Italy)

Germany claimed third place.

> **Stat Attack**
>
> The 1934 tournament had the lowest average attendance of any World Cup, with little over 23,000 on average attending each match.

World Cup Final

In the Stadium of the National Fascist Party in Rome, Benito Mussolini watched on as his **Italy** side were again forced to perform the fascist salute prior to their meeting with **Czechoslovakia**, the winner of which would be crowned world champions. It proved an intriguing contest. The Czechs were the quicker out of the blocks and went about trying to put together their neat attacking game, while Italy's enforcer Luis Monti did his level best to disrupt their rhythm. As the game wore on, however, the Czechs forced their way into the game more and more. They deserved a goal for their performance and finally found one with quarter of an hour remaining. Outside left Antonin Puc, a thorn in the Italians' side all day, was the provider, taking a corner, receiving the ball back and letting fly from long range, deceiving the unsighted Azzurri keeper Giampiero Combi as the ball flew past him to spark pandemonium in the stands. Czechoslovakia were just minutes away from claiming a title they richly deserved in their opponents' hostile lions' den. They went in search of the clincher as the stunned Italians watched on. Centre forward Jiri Sobotka looked certain to score after being put through but fired wastefully wide before fellow striker Frantisek Svoboda also had a fantastic chance to put the Czechs out of sight but crashed a vicious shot off the post with Combi hopelessly beaten. Then, out of nowhere, Italy stole an undeserved equaliser thanks to a moment of genius from their Argentinean left winger Raimundo Orsi. The wide man cut inside, slipping through several Czech challenges, dummied a shot with his favoured left boot before catching out Frantisek Planicka in the Czechoslovakia goal with an outrageous swerving shot from range blasted off the outside of his right foot which left the Czech captain grasping only air. Inevitably this late equaliser, scored utterly against the run of play, deflated the Czechs and gave encouragement to the Italians. Backed by their passionate crowd, they gained a foothold in extra time and scored the winner when Meazza's cross picked out another Argentinean, Enrique Guaita, who fed Angelo Schiavio for the centre forward to compose himself and lash beyond Planicka. Much to the delight of Mussolini and his government, Italy were world champions. They could count themselves most fortunate, however, the Czechs having dominated for 90 minutes but coming away with nothing to show for their inspired performance.

> **Only at the World Cup**
>
> Italy left half Luigi Bertolini is easily recognisable in pictures of the final: he wore a massive white headband to protect from injury.

> **Only at the World Cup**
>
> The pressure from Mussolini's fascist government for Italy to win the tournament was huge, as was the fear of failure for the Azzurri as a result. This was illustrated by match-winner Schiavio explaining his goal by saying "the strength of desperation" had made him score!

> **Only at the World Cup**
>
> Italy's hero Orsi allegedly returned the following day so photographers could take a picture of him replicating his equalising goal! Try as he might, however, he could not repeat it! So not a fluke at all then Raimundo!

World Cup Final result

Italy 2-1 Czechoslovakia (aet)
10/06/34 – Rome (Stadio Nazionale PNF)
Italy: Combi (c), Monzeglio, Allemandi, Ferraris, Monti, Bertolini, Guaita, Meazza, Schiavio, Ferrari, Orsi
Goals: Orsi 81, Schiavio 95
Czechoslovakia: Planicka (c), Zenisek, Ctyroky, Kostalek, Cambal, Krcil, Junek, Svoboda, Sobotka, Nejedly, Puc
Goals: Puc 76
Referee: Eklind (Sweden)

Italy won the 1934 World Cup.

Tournament awards

Golden Boot: Oldrich Nejedly (Czechoslovakia) – 5 goals
(Runners-up: Angelo Schiavio (Italy)/Edmund Conen (Germany) – 4)

Best Player: Giuseppe Meazza (Italy)

Best Goal: Raimundo Orsi (Italy) – An outrageous piece of individual skill in the final, cutting through challenges, dummying a shot and curling home a screamer with the outside of his weaker foot. Fluke it may have been but we'll give you the benefit of the doubt Raimundo!

Star XI:
Goalkeeper – Ricardo Zamora (Spain)
Defenders – Jacinto Quincoces (Spain), Luigi Allemandi (Italy)
Midfielders – Fritz Szepan (Germany), Luis Monti (Italy), Luigi Bertolini (Italy)
Forwards – Enrique Guaita (Italy), Giuseppe Meazza (Italy), Matthias Sindelar (Austria), Oldrich Nejedly (Czechoslovakia), Raimundo Orsi (Italy)

World Cup Great – Luis Monti (Argentina and Italy)

Nowadays, the idea that a player could have a successful international career with one country and then go on and play for another is ludicrous but for much of the 20th century it was fairly common. Still, very few players enjoyed genuine success with two different countries. One of the few who did, and one of the best of all, was Argentina and Italy's dominant centre half Luisito Monti.

Monti began his career at Argentinean club Huracan in 1921 and would help his side to the league title that season. He was soon snapped up by top club Boca Juniors but would actually never play for them, instead moving on again soon after, this time to San Lorenzo, where he would spend some of the best days of his career. In his time at the club he would win a further three Argentinean titles and establish himself in the national side, winning his first cap in 1924.

Monti became the heartbeat of the Argentina side, responsible for dealing, often brutally, with the opponent's centre forward before starting attacks from deep. Monti was brilliant at this role and helped his side to the final of the 1928 Olympics, only to lose to reigning champions Uruguay. Monti and Argentina would be back for the first World Cup two years later. The midfield enforcer was at his brilliant best in the tournament, scoring twice on the way to the final. He was most noticeable, as always, for the uncompromising way he would deal with his opponents, showing them no quarter as he brutally knocked them down. One of the first masters of the dark arts of defending, Monti was soon feared the world over.

Perhaps it was this brutal tackling, which caused him to injure several players in the tournament, that resulted in the Uruguayan public singling him out for particular hatred prior to the final, with one even sending him a death threat. As it happened, even Monti's aggression and skill couldn't stop Argentina going down 4-2 to the hosts. Nevertheless, Monti's performances attracted the attention of top Italian side Juventus, who signed him the following year. The veteran centre half soon became the cornerstone of his new club, helping them to four successive league titles. He was soon also a regular for the Italian national team. At the age of 33, he was the key player in Italy's legendary midfield with Attilio Ferraris and Luigi Bertolini and one of the stars of the 1934 World Cup. Reaching his second final, the only man to play in two World Cup finals for two different teams, he finally won the trophy with victory over Czechoslovakia.

Monti played very much as a modern-day holding midfielder would, a ferocious and brutal tackler in defence but able to play superb passes out from deep. Argentina and Italy have both produced a host of successors to Monti but arguably none have matched his combination of tackling power and passing ability. His legacy in Argentina is so great that the "number five" is still the key component of the side.

The first World Cup in Europe had generally been a successful affair but, just as in Uruguay four years earlier, the dominance of the teams from the home continent had been complete. In this case, it had been so great that all eight quarter-finalists were European, the only time this would ever occur. This utter domination made the tournament too predictable at times, but at least the football had been exciting.

Of course the major talking point of the tournament would be Italy's triumph on home soil and the controversial politics that surrounded it. There could be little doubt that Italy boasted a team full of stars and had been simply untouchable at times but at the same time there had also been no doubt that, under pressure from Mussolini and the country's fascist government, several referees had been intimidated into making shockingly biased decisions. The worst of these cases undoubtedly came in their two games with Spain, the first seeing Spanish keeper Ricardo Zamora repeatedly fouled and eventually injured, the second, even worse, containing a shocking winner, Spanish goals wrongly disallowed and more horrendous fouls. The result was that Spain, a fine side in their own right, were denied the chance to have their own shot at the title.

Austria, meanwhile, had been a big disappointment. Tipped to be Italy's closest challengers, the Wunderteam never really found their form, coasting into the semis at half pace and being unable to raise their game to see off the hosts. Instead, it had been left to Czechoslovakia to play the tournament's best football. Inspired by the free-scoring Nejedly, the Czechs were the better side in all their games and were desperately unlucky to lose to Italy in the final, with more unpleasant undertones from Mussolini and co. In truth, Italy's first World Cup was certainly a tainted victory but to blame the players for matters out of their control and not of their asking would be incredibly harsh. Whether or not Mussolini's government had bribed officials, as is often alleged, it still takes little away from the performances on the pitch of the team and the individual players.

1938: France

Qualification

37 Entrants.
Italy qualified as holders.
France qualified as hosts.

Spain withdrew before draw was made as a result of ongoing civil war.

Group 1

Sweden 4-0 Finland, Sweden 7-2 Estonia, Finland 0-2 Germany, Finland 0-1 Estonia, Germany 4-1 Estonia, Germany 5-0 Sweden

	Pld	W	D	L	GF	GA	Pts
Germany	3	3	0	0	11	1	6
Sweden	3	2	0	1	11	7	4
Estonia	3	1	0	2	4	11	2
Finland	3	0	0	3	0	7	0

Germany and **Sweden** qualified.

Group 2

Norway 3-2 Ireland, Ireland 3-3 Norway

	Pld	W	D	L	GF	GA	Pts
Norway	2	1	1	0	6	5	3
Ireland	2	0	1	1	5	6	1

Norway qualified.

Group 3

Poland 4-0 Yugoslavia, Yugoslavia 1-0 Poland

	Pld	W	D	L	GF	GA	Pts
Poland	2	1	0	1	4	1	2
Yugoslavia	2	1	0	1	1	4	2

Poland qualified.

Group 4

Egypt withdrew.

Romania qualified.

Group 5

Switzerland 2-1 Portugal (in Italy)

Switzerland qualified.

Group 6

Palestine v Greece: 1-3, 0-1 (agg. 1-4)
Hungary 11-1 Greece

Hungary qualified.

Group 7

Bulgaria 1-1 Czechoslovakia, Czechoslovakia 6-0 Bulgaria

	Pld	W	D	L	GF	GA	Pts
Czechoslovakia	2	1	1	0	7	1	3
Bulgaria	2	0	1	1	1	7	1

Czechoslovakia qualified.

Group 8

Latvia v Lithuania: 4-2, 5-1 (agg. 9-3)
Austria 2-1 Latvia

Austria qualified but were forced to withdraw after they were annexed by Germany. England, who had not competed in the qualifiers, were offered a place but declined, leaving the tournament one team short.

> **Only at the World Cup**
>
> Only 15 teams competed in the 1938 World Cup because Nazi Germany annexed Austria, casually helping themselves to their best players and forcing them to withdraw! What kind neighbours those Nazis were!

Group 9

Holland 4-0 Luxembourg, Luxembourg 2-3 Belgium, Belgium 1-1 Holland

	Pld	W	D	L	GF	GA	Pts
Holland	2	1	1	0	5	1	3
Belgium	2	1	1	0	4	3	3
Luxembourg	2	0	0	2	2	7	0

Holland and **Belgium** qualified.

Group 10

Argentina withdrew.

Brazil qualified.

Group 11

USA, Mexico, El Salvador, Costa Rica, Dutch Guiana and Colombia withdrew.

Cuba qualified.

Group 12

Japan withdrew.

Dutch East Indies qualified.

> **Only at the World Cup**
>
> The decision to host the competition in France incensed the Americas and as a result many of their teams pulled out. The mighty Dutch Guiana would not be strutting their stuff in France after all then!

> **Stat Attack**
>
> The Dutch East Indies (modern day Indonesia) were the first Asian side to qualify for the tournament. This would be the country's only World Cup appearance to date, however.

The Contenders

Belgium	Hungary
Brazil	Italy
Cuba	Norway
Czechoslovakia	Poland
Dutch East Indies	Romania
France	Sweden
Germany	Switzerland
Holland	Austria (withdrawn)

France were chosen as the third World Cup hosts ahead of Argentina and the dubious option of Nazi Germany by a landslide decision but this was not a move that proved popular all around the world. The South American nations, expecting the tournament to alternate between the two continents, were furious with the selection of a second successive European host, leading Argentina, Uruguay and a host of other countries in the Americas to boycott the event in anger. The result was another tournament consisting almost wholly of European teams.

As the qualifying games had been played, the storm clouds over Europe had been gradually darkening. Spain had been forced to withdraw as early as 1936 as a violent civil war tore their country apart, while the threat of equally bloody war was looming large over the continent. Indeed, Hitler's expansionist Nazi Germany had annexed Austria in Anschluss months before the tournament began, leaving just 15 teams in the competition, as the Germans took Austria's best players for their own side. The 1938 World Cup would be played in an atmosphere of fear and suspicion.

Despite Austria's withdrawal, the knockout system used in Italy four years earlier would be retained, granting Sweden, who had been fortunate enough to draw Austria days before their enforced withdrawal, a bye into the quarter-finals. Just four wins could be sufficient to win the World Cup, with replays again used if teams were level at the end of 30 minutes of extra time.

Reigning champions **Italy**, who had added the 1936 Olympic title to their World Cup victory on home soil in 1934, were favourites to retain the trophy. Mastermind coach Vittorio Pozzo was still present and confident he could again lead his charges to triumph. Key men were also still available from four years earlier, most notably playmaker Giuseppe Meazza, now the captain, and his inside forward partner Giovanni Ferrari. Added to these players' experience were exciting new discoveries, including devastating centre forward Silvio Piola and accomplished defenders Alfredo Foni and Pietro Rava. They would unquestionably be the team to beat in France.

Czechoslovakia, so unlucky to lose to Italy in the final four years earlier, would also return. Like Italy, several of their best players remained. Still able to call on the varied talents of Frantisek Planicka in goal, Oldrich Nejedly up front and Antonin Puc on the wing, many felt they were well equipped to go one better and win the tournament this time around. That said, they had been hammered 8-3 by **Hungary** in September 1937. Such a clinical performance also put the Hungarians among the very first tier of favourites. They retained the skills of Gyorgy Sarosi and he would now be helped in the goalscoring department by gifted inside left Gyula Zsengeller.

Meanwhile, **France** would be looking to continue the tradition established by the first two World Cups of the hosts winning the tournament. However, they looked by far the least likely of the three to accomplish the feat, given they had a far from exceptional side. They could still call upon the skills of striker Jean Nicolas and the experience at the back of Etienne Mattler but for them to carry off the title would require a superhuman performance. **Germany**, meanwhile, who had bid against France in their hopes to host the tournament themselves, seemed to have a much better chance of victory. Galvanised by the presence of Austria's finest (though the best of all, Matthias Sindelar, had refused to take part), they had ability and strength in depth, while experienced midfield duo Paul Janes and Fritz Szepan were still present. A serious challenge looked likely.

Brazil may have been the only South American team in the tournament but at least this time they promised much. A fast-improving footballing nation, the Brazilians were finally beginning to make their mark on the international stage, with brilliant young striker Leonidas their star. Allied to the defensive talents of Domingos da Guia, Brazil had two fantastic bookends to base their team around. That both these star men were black also spoke volumes about the development of Brazilian football, which had barely a decade earlier been renowned for racist selection.

None of the other sides in the tournament looked likely victors but they still came with hopes of making their mark on the competition. **Switzerland** were probably the best of the rest, with forwards Andre Abegglen and Leopold Kielholz returning after their successes in Italy four years previously. **Sweden**, meanwhile, would also come with every chance, especially given that they would automatically reach the quarter-finals thanks to Austria's withdrawal. Dangerous forward Sven Jonasson would return and he would be assisted by the pace of winger Gustav Wetterstrom. **Romania** and **Belgium** would both also come full of experience, thanks to two previous World Cup appearances. For the Romanians, Nicolae Covaci would again be present while another 1930 veteran, Ladislau Raffinsky, would also return after missing the intervening competition. Belgium, meanwhile, could yet again call on the goalscoring talents of Bernard Voorhoof, for whom this would be a third successive World Cup.

Holland would also not lack experience with Puck Van Heel, Kick Smit and Leen Vente among a gaggle of players who played in Italy four years earlier. However, facing Czechoslovakia in the first round would be a monstrous task. An even greater one was in store for debutants **Norway**, who would have to deal with the reigning champions in their opening match. Outside left Arne Brustad would be the key man for an emerging football nation who had surprised everyone by taking the bronze medal in the 1936 Berlin Olympics. **Poland**, like Norway, would also be playing in their first ever World Cup, having seen off Yugoslavia in qualifying. Prolific striker Ernst Willimowski, whose absence had been so keenly felt in the 1936 Olympics, would be back to terrorise defences and he gave the Poles every chance of making a real impact on tournament proceedings.

The tournament's two biggest outsiders were the intriguing pair of **Cuba** and the **Dutch East Indies**. Both had qualified without playing a game thanks to the withdrawal of other sides. Both came almost entirely unknown to the Europeans and would relish their big chance on the world stage.

Debutants: Cuba, Dutch East Indies, Norway, Poland

The Draw

Germany v Switzerland
Hungary v Dutch East Indies
Sweden v (Austria)
Cuba v Romania
France v Belgium
Italy v Norway
Brazil v Poland
Czechoslovakia v Holland

> **Stat Attack**
>
> Lyon's Stade Gerland became the only World Cup venue not to host a match after the only game scheduled for it, Austria's clash with Sweden, was cancelled when the former withdrew.

Venues:
Paris – Olympique de Colombes, Paris – Parc des Princes, Antibes, Bordeaux, Le Havre, Lille, Lyon, Marseille, Reims, Strasbourg, Toulouse

The Tournament – 4-19 June

First Round

The tournament opened at the Parc des Princes in Paris, where **Germany**, boasting several Austrians in their starting line-up, took on **Switzerland**. The Germans, fortified by the addition of their Austrian contingent, started the stronger and had a deserved lead to celebrate just before the half hour. Hans Pesser, one of the Austrians on the field, crossed from the left for Jupp Gauchel to fire past the Swiss keeper. Many thought this might have been the cue for the combined might of Greater Germany to flex their muscles but instead Switzerland fought back, Andre Abegglen providing their equaliser with a header at the very end of the first half. From then on, there were 75 minutes of goalless football, right up until the end of extra time. They were certainly not without chances, however, both teams failing to take opportunities to win the game and Pesser, a hero earlier in the game, ruining his good performance by being sent off for a violent foul. A replay a few days later would be needed to settle the tie.

The competition's next four matches all took place simultaneously the following day. In one of them, debutants the **Dutch East Indies** faced the considerable task of attempting to beat a top-class **Hungary** side in Reims. Predictably, their opposition and the occasion proved well beyond them and they were on the receiving end of a convincing beating. The Hungarian forward line had a field day, helping themselves to a clutch of goal to get themselves in the scoring appetite for tougher challenges later in the tournament. The game was all over by half-time, Vilmos Kohut and Geza Toldi setting the Europeans on their way before Gyorgy Sarosi and Gyula Zsengeller got in on the act too, 4-0 after 45 minutes. At least for the thoroughly outplayed debutants the Hungarians relaxed somewhat in the second half with the security of a four-goal lead, although they did twice extend it late on, Zsengeller and Sarosi both grabbing their second goals of the game to heap further misery on the poor Asians. Hungary were through in style while the Dutch East Indies' dream day had turned into something of a nightmare.

Fellow minnows **Cuba** were also in action that afternoon, taking on **Romania** in Toulouse. However, this match would see a very different performance and outcome. There looked little prospect of what was to come when Silvio Bindea put the Europeans in front after 38 minutes. However, Cuba used their pace in attack to thoroughly unsettle the Romanians, Hector Socorro equalising before half-time. Sensationally, Cuba then proceeded to take the lead, Tomas Fernandez firing home after another quick attack. Shocked, Romania appeared to be going out but scrambled home an equaliser in the dying moments, Iuliu Baratky finally getting the ball in the net. Extra time came next but neither side could take the chance of a winner, though both added one more goal, Bindea scoring his second for the Europeans and Juan Tunas gratefully finding the net for the Caribbean side. Incredibly, tiny Cuba had forced a replay with one of Europe's established footballing nations.

Meanwhile, hosts **France** got their campaign under way at the Stade Olympique de Colombes in Paris, with neighbours **Belgium** their opponents. The home crowd were desperate for an early nerve settler and they got it amazingly after just 35 seconds, Emile Veinante firing beyond Arnold Badjou from close range. France continued to dominate and added a second 15 minutes later, star centre forward Jean Nicolas giving the French some breathing space. If the fans thought this would be a simple stroll to victory, however, they were mistaken as Belgium found their form and began to dominate the game. Henri Isemborghs finished off a well-constructed attack to pull it back to 2-1 and Laurent Di Lorto in the French goal was called upon several times to rescue his side, his smart goalkeeping ensuring France stayed ahead. Weathering their sticky patch, Les Bleus made sure of it 20 minutes from time, Alfred Aston, a dangerous presence all game, crossing from the right and Nicolas firing an exquisite first-time shot with his right foot which flew into the top corner. Paris could rejoice as the home side were delivered safely to the quarter-finals.

Italy too got their title defence under way at the same time, facing unfancied debutants **Norway** in Marseille. It seemed set for a gentle way to ease Italy into the tournament but in the end it proved far from it. Pietro Ferraris put the champions ahead in the opening exchanges but it proved a false dawn, as the Norwegians, free from the pressure of expectation, tore into their more illustrious opponents. Only the brilliance of Aldo Olivieri in the Italian goal could deny the Scandinavians as he produced a succession of stunning saves to halt the endless waves of Norwegian attacks, his goal frame also coming to the rescue several times as Italy failed to rise to the challenge. Inevitably, Olivieri was finally beaten minutes before the end, Arne Brustad scoring the goal his performance deserved to send Italy into shock. However, the Azzurri finally remembered why they were world champions in extra time, going on the offensive and scoring a scrappy winner when Henry Johansen failed to hold a shot and the lurking Silvio Piola tapped home. Brave Norway were finally beaten but they had played brilliantly to massively enhance their reputation. Italy, meanwhile, could count themselves extremely fortunate to have survived. If they harboured ambitions of retaining their title, they would have to improve and fast.

> **Only at the World Cup**
>
> Italy's opening game with Norway saw one of the most controversial incidents of any World Cup. The Italian team were ordered to perform the fascist salute before the match but were severely jeered by the crowd, causing them to lower their arms. However, coach Vittorio Pozzo ordered them to continue the salute until the jeers died down so as to "win the intimidation." Perhaps in hindsight it was not the greatest way to make friends!

Two further matches would take place later that day. The first of these was a veritable goal feast in Strasbourg, still considered to this day by some to be the greatest World Cup match of all time. It proved a clash between two top-class teams committed to attacking football: **Brazil** and **Poland**. It would also be a meeting of two world-class strikers at the top of their game: Leonidas and Ernst Willimowski. It was the former who put Brazil in front 18 minutes in but rather than spark any manner of control, this was merely the cue for an avalanche of goals. Indeed, an astonishing 11 would be scored in the game. The second of these was a penalty converted by Poland's Friedrich Scherfke after Willimowski, causing havoc with his pace and determination, was disgracefully hauled to the ground in what was almost a rugby tackle! However, goals from Leonidas' attacking counterparts Romeu and Peracio put the South Americans 3-1 up at half-time. However, the fun was only just getting started and Willimowski was about to show just how devastating he could be. Time and again he tore the Brazilian defence to ribbons and with an hour gone, he had scored twice to pull things back to 3-3. The Brazilians rallied again, however, Peracio scoring his second to re-establish their lead and they looked to be going through until Willimowski came again to the Poles' rescue, completing his hat-trick with seconds remaining to take the game into extra time. With the score already 4-4, it had been quite some game but that would not be the end of this carnival of goals. Leonidas, who had started off the fun in the first place, got back in on the act, scoring twice more to register a hat-trick of his own and put Brazil back on course for the win. Still, Willimowski refused to give up, scoring his fourth goal of the game with two minutes remaining to leave the South Americans sweating all the way to the final whistle. Finishing 6-5, it had been an astonishing game and a joy to watch for those fortunate enough to have attended. Exhausted they might be but Brazil could bask in the warm glow created by their astonishing victory. For poor Poland, there was dejection but they could take immense pride from their performance in the match.

Finally, **Czechoslovakia** took on **Holland** in Le Havre. The Czechs, expected to win with ease, made remarkably heavy weather of their limited opponents. Puck Van Heel and his defensive colleagues were brilliant for 90 minutes as they frustrated the Czechs' skilful attackers. However, they were able to offer very little threat of their own up front and their failure to trouble Planicka would prove costly as the game entered extra time. Finally, the Czechs ran riot over the exhausted Dutch, Josef Kostalek, Oldrich Nejedly and Josef Zeman all scoring in the additional 30 minutes to secure victory. However, there was no doubt they had been made to work hard by the steadfastness of Holland's defending.

> **Stat Attack**
>
> Poland's Ernst Willimowski became the first player to score four goals in a World Cup match. However, he still ended up on the losing side, though he is the only ever World Cup player to score so many goals but still taste defeat.

With two ties ending level after extra time, replays were organised three days before the quarter-final dates to determine the last two entrants of that stage. **Germany** and **Switzerland** faced each other again in one of the **replay**s and most expected a simple German victory. This appeared to be the way the game was heading midway through the first half as the Germans took a 2-0 lead, Wilhelm Hahnemann opening the scoring and the luckless Ernst Lortscher compounding the Swiss problems with an unfortunate own goal. However, Switzerland weren't about to throw in the towel and they had hope by half-time when Eugen Walaschek reduced the arrears. Still, few gave them hope of mounting an incredible comeback but that was what they managed, weathering a barrage of German attacks throughout the second period to occasionally hit out decisively on the counterattack, Alfred Bickel equalising before Andre Abegglen broke German hearts with two late

> **Stat Attack**
>
> Switzerland half-back Ernst Lortscher scored the first ever World Cup own goal in his country's 4-2 win over Germany.

goals. Incredibly, the Swiss had fashioned a remarkable comeback to eliminate the fancied Germans and take their place in the World Cup quarter-finals.

The other **replay** saw **Romania** seek an improved performance against little **Cuba**, who had caused them such unexpected problems four days earlier. Incredibly, the Romanians made exactly the same mistakes again in Toulouse, somehow managing to still underestimate their spirited opposition. Again they took the lead, this time Stefan Dobai pouncing to put them in front and in control at half-time. However, again they sat back and let the speedy Cuban attackers hassle them. The hugely impressive Hector Socorro equalised and then, sensationally, Carlos Oliveira put them in front. There was still plenty of time for Romania to come back but, stunned, they had no answer. Astonishingly, Cuba had beaten Romania and struck a blow to the heart of European football. They would compete in the quarter-finals.

> **Only at the World Cup**
>
> Tiny Cuba shocked the world by beating Romania to reach the quarter-finals, easily the biggest World Cup upset in the inter-war period. Sadly, lads, you're about to find out it's all downhill from here!

First Round results

Germany 1-1 Switzerland (aet)
04/06/38 – Paris (Parc des Princes)
Germany: Raftl, Janes, Schmaus, Kupfer, Mock (c), Kitzinger, Lehner, Gellesch, Gauchel, Hahnemann, Pesser
Goals: Gauchel 29
Sent off: Pesser 96
Switzerland: Huber, Minelli (c), Lehmann, Springer, Vernati, Lortscher, Amado, Walaschek, Bickel, Abegglen, G Aeby
Goals: Abegglen 43
Referee: Langenus (Belgium)

Hungary 6-0 Dutch East Indies
05/06/38 – Reims (Municipal)
Hungary: Hada, Koranyi, S Biro, Lazar, Turay, Balogh, Sas, Zsengeller, G Sarosi (c), Toldi, Kohut
Goals: Kohut 13, Toldi 15, Sarosi 28, 89, Zsengeller 35, 76
Dutch East Indies: Tan Mo Heng, Hu Kon, Samuels, Nawir (c), Meeng, Anwar, Hong Djien, Soedarmadji, Zomers, Pattiwael, Taihuttu
Referee: Conrie (France)

Cuba 3-3 Romania (aet)
05/06/38 – Toulouse (Chapou)
Cuba: Carvajales, Barquin, Chorens, Arias, Rodriguez, Berges (c), Oliveira, Fernandez, Socorro, Tunas, Sosa
Goals: Socorro 41, Fernandez 61, Tunas 101
Romania: Pavlovici, Burger, Chiroiu, Cossini, Rasinaru, Raffinsky, Bindea, Covaci (c), Baratki, Bodola, Dobai
Goals: Bindea 38, 93, Baratki 88
Referee: Scarpi (Italy)

France 3-1 Belgium
05/06/38 – Paris (Colombes)
France: Di Lorto, Cazenave, Mattler (c), Bastien, Jordan, Diagne, Aston, Heisserer, Nicolas, Delfour, Veinante
Goals: Veinante 1, Nicolas 16, 69
Belgium: Badjou, Paverick, Seys, Van Alphen, Stynen (c), De Winter, Van de Wouwer, Voorhoof, Isemborghs, R Braine, Buyle
Goals: Isemborghs 38
Referee: Wuthrich (Switzerland)

Italy 2-1 Norway (aet)
05/06/38 – Marseille (Velodrome)
Italy: Olivieri, Monzeglio, Rava, Serantoni, Andreolo, Locatelli, Pasinati, Meazza (c), Piola, Ferrari, P Ferraris
Goals: P Ferraris 2, Piola 94
Norway: Johansen, Johannesen, Holmsen, Henriksen, Eriksen (c), Holmberg, Frantzen, Kvammen, Brynildsen, Isaksen, Brustad
Goals: Brustad 83
Referee: Beranek (Austria)

Brazil 6-5 Poland (aet)
05/06/38 – Strasbourg (La Meinau)
Brazil: Batatais, Domingos, Machado, Zeze Procopio, Martim Silveira (c), Afonsinho, Lopes, Romeu, Leonidas, Peracio, Hercules
Goals: Leonidas 18, 93, 104, Romeu 25, Peracio 44, 71
Poland: Madejski, Szczepaniak (c), Galecki, Gora, Nyc, Dytko, R Piec, Piontek, Scherfke, Willimowski, Wodarz
Goals: Scherfke pen 23, Willimowski 53, 59, 89, 118
Referee: Eklind (Sweden)

Czechoslovakia 3-0 Holland (aet)
05/06/38 – Le Havre (Cavee Verte)
Czechoslovakia: Planicka (c), Burgr, Daucik, Kostalek, Boucek, Kopecky, Riha, Simunek, Zeman, Nejedly, Puc
Goals: Kostalek 93, Nejedly 111, Zeman 118
Holland: Van Male, Weber, Caldenhove, Paauwe, Anderiesen, Van Heel (c), Wels, Van der Veen, Smit, Vente, de Harder
Referee: Leclerq (France)

Replays

Germany 2-4 Switzerland
09/06/38 – Paris (Parc des Princes)
Germany: Raftl, Janes, Streitle, Kupfer, Goldbrunner, Skoumal, Lehner, Stroh, Szepan (c), Hahnemann, Neumer
Goals: Hahnemann 8, Lortscher (og) 22
Switzerland: Huber, Minelli (c), Lehmann, Springer, Vernati, Lortscher, Amado, Walaschek, Bickel, Abegglen, G Aeby
Goals: Walaschek 42, Bickel 64, Abegglen 75, 78
Referee: Eklind (Sweden)

Cuba 2-1 Romania
09/06/38 – Toulouse (Chapou)
Cuba: Ayra, Barquin, Chorens, Arias, Rodriguez, Berges (c), Oliveira, Fernandez, Socorro, Tunas, Sosa
Goals: Socorro 51, Oliveira 53
Romania: Sadowski, Burger, Felecan, Barbulescu, Rasinaru, Raffinsky, Bogdan, Moldoveanu, Baratki, Prassler, Dobai (c)
Goals: Dobai 28
Referee: Birlem (Germany)

Switzerland, Hungary, Sweden, Cuba, France, Italy, Brazil and Czechoslovakia qualified for quarter-finals.

> **Only at the World Cup**
>
> Austria's withdrawal meant Sweden progressed without playing a game. There probably weren't too many complaints in the Swedish camp!

Quarter-finals

Switzerland, still exhausted from their ultra-competitive replay with Germany, were predictably too fatigued to put up much of a fight in Lille against a far fresher **Hungary**, whose comfortable stroll against the Dutch East Indies had been far less tiring preparation. The Hungarians were able to use their greater fitness to run rings round the exhausted Swiss, who simply had no answer to their greater pace and speed of thought. Inevitably, Hungary took the lead through a Gyorgy Sarosi header and held it comfortably. To their credit, Switzerland never capitulated but there looked little prospect of them getting level once they fell behind. Gyula Zsengeller finished them with a second goal at the death. Fatigue had accounted for the brave Swiss and Hungary would compete in their first World Cup semi-final.

If Switzerland were no match for Hungary it was nothing compared to the fresh legs of **Sweden**, yet to play a single minute of football in the tournament, taking on the shattered bodies of **Cuba** the same day in Antibes. The Cubans had played their World Cup final in the incredible victory over Romania and had nothing left in the tank. In the circumstances, they simply fell apart, the Scandinavians obliterating them 8-0. Their captain Tore Keller put them in front early on and from then on it was virtually one-way traffic. Gustav Wetterstrom fired in a hat-trick in just 12 first-half minutes for a 4-0 lead at the break, Cuba having their only chance when Tomas Fernandez saw a penalty attempt saved by Henock Abrahamsson. Well beaten already, the Cubans simply went to pieces in the final ten minutes of the game, allowing Sweden to score a further four goals, Keller notching two in a minute to complete his own hat-trick before fellow forwards Arne Nyberg and Harry Andersson got in on the act with strikes of their own. Cuba had pulled off a fairytale result earlier but this was the grim reality of World Cup football. The Swedes, meanwhile, had coasted into the semi-finals without playing even a minute of truly competitive football. The draw had been more than a little kind to their largely average side.

The most anticipated match of the quarter-finals took place at the Stade Olympique de Colombes in Paris where hosts **France** took on holders **Italy**. The Italians came into the game in dreadful form and there was a sense among the home crowd that France might have a chance. They faced an early wave of attacks from the Italians, however, and goalkeeper Laurent Di Lorto had to be alert several times to snuff out the danger. However, it was a horrendous error from Di Lorto that resulted in Italy's opening goal. A well-worked attack ended in Gino Colaussi, brought in on the left wing, lobbing in a shot which looked comfortable for Di Lorto only for the back-pedalling keeper to limply palm it into his own net. Undeterred, the French hit back a minute later, Alfred Aston and Jean Nicolas combining brilliantly to release Oscar Heisserer, who fired powerfully past Aldo Olivieri. For the rest of the first half, the two sides sparred cautiously and it looked like being anyone's game. However, ever-alert centre forward Silvio Piola had other ideas, putting paid to French hopes with two well-taken second-half goals. France were out and would not add to the record of the previous two World Cups, where the hosts had won on both occasions. Italy, on the other hand, looked to be firmly back on track.

> **Only at the World Cup**
>
> Italy, fresh from the fascist salute furore of their opening game, chose to further antagonise the crowd and intimidate their opponents by taking the field decked out entirely in black, a deliberately fascist kit. Or maybe they just thought they looked great in black!

Throughout the history of the World Cup, the competition has occasionally been marred by games where both sides have resorted to sickening acts of violence and all premise of playing football has been lost. The first such game in World Cup history took place in 1938 in the "Battle of Bordeaux" between **Brazil** and **Czechoslovakia**. The game seemed to promise much, as both sides played highly attractive attacking football and were among the very best teams in the world. However, this game will always be remembered as a spectacle for all the wrong reasons. The game burst into life when Brazil half-back Zeze Procopio was the first of three players sent off, and this after only 14 minutes. Both teams soon resorted to viciously kicking and fouling one another at every opportunity, with the South Americans the chief offenders. Amidst all this, Leonidas put Brazil in front but yet another Brazilian foul allowed Oldrich Nejedly to equalise from the penalty spot. However, the result of all this brutality was, sadly, some sickening injuries. Worst of all was to see star Czechoslovakia forward Nejedly stretchered off with a horrific broken leg. There was more to come as Brazilian forward Peracio followed through a shot with a vicious kick to break keeper Frantisek Planicka's arm, though scandalously the player went unpunished! Planicka heroically remained on the field, even throughout the extra time that resulted, courageously defying the Brazilians. Meanwhile, both sides lost another player to indiscipline, Machado and Jan Riha sent off for fighting. In the end, with the actual game often a secondary consideration to the horrors going on all around, the match ended 1-1. A replay would be needed and hopefully there would be no repeat of the shocking violence on display.

> **Only at the World Cup**
>
> Brazil's game with Czechoslovakia was a horror show of sickening tackles and petulant fighting which saw two horrific injuries and three players sent off, a record that would not be exceeded in a World Cup match for 68 years! I'm sure you're all gutted you didn't see that one then!

Two days after the horrors of their first match, **Brazil** and **Czechoslovakia** faced each other once again in a **replay**. Given the nature of the game that had gone before, it was hardly surprising that both sides were missing several players through injury. The Czechs were by far the worst affected, with key trio Planicka, Nejedly and Puc all out. Nevertheless, it was the European side who took the lead, Vlastimil Kopecky firing home. With both sides thankfully concentrating on the game, the Czechs seemed to be gaining the upper hand but Leonidas had other ideas, the deadly centre forward equalising before Roberto scored to send Brazil deliriously through to the World Cup semi-finals for the first time. For the poor Czechs, they would live to rue the brutal clash two days earlier, though even missing their best players they had run the South Americans close and had proved themselves a world-class side.

Quarter-final results

Switzerland 0-2 Hungary
12/06/38 – Lille (Victor Boucquey)
Switzerland: Huber, Stelzer, Lehmann (c), Springer, Vernati, Lortscher, Amado, Walaschek, Bickel, Abegglen, Grassi
Hungary: A Szabo, Koranyi, S Biro, Lazar, Turay, Szalay, Sas, Vincze, G Sarosi (c), Zsengeller, Kohut
Goals: G Sarosi 40, Zsengeller 89
Referee: Barlassina (Italy)

Sweden 8-0 Cuba
12/06/38 – Antibes (Stade du Fort Carre)
Sweden: Abrahamsson, Eriksson, Kallgren, Almgren, Jacobsson, Svanstrom, Wetterstrom, Keller (c), H Andersson, Jonasson, Nyberg
Goals: Keller 9, 80, 81, Wetterstrom 32, 37, 44, Nyberg 84, H Andersson 90
Cuba: Carvajales, Barquin, Chorens, Arias, Rodriguez, Berges (c), Ferrer, Fernandez, Socorro, Tunas, Alonso
Referee: Krist (Czechoslovakia)

France 1-3 Italy
12/06/38 – Paris (Colombes)
France: Di Lorto, Cazenave, Mattler (c), Bastien, Jordan, Diagne, Aston, Heisserer, Nicolas, Delfour, Veinante
Goals: Heisserer 10
Italy: Olivieri, Foni, Rava, Serantoni, Andreolo, Locatelli, Biavati, Meazza (c), Piola, Ferrari, Colaussi
Goals: Colaussi 9, Piola 51, 72
Referee: Baert (Belgium)

Brazil 1-1 Czechoslovakia (aet)
12/06/38 – Bordeaux (Parc Lescure)
Brazil: Walter, Domingos, Machado, Zeze Procopio, Martim Silveira (c), Afonsinho, Lopes, Romeu, Leonidas, Peracio, Hercules
Goals: Leonidas 30
Sent off: Zeze Procopio 14, Machado 89
Czechoslovakia: Planicka (c), Burgr, Daucik, Kostalek, Boucek, Kopecky, Riha, Simunek, Ludl, Nejedly, Puc
Goals: Nejedly pen 65
Sent off: Riha 89
Referee: Von Hertzka (Hungary)

Replay

Brazil 2-1 Czechoslovakia
14/06/38 – Bordeaux (Parc Lescure)
Brazil: Walter, Jau, Nariz, Britto, Brandao, Argemiro, Roberto, Luizinho, Leonidas (c), Tim, Patesko
Goals: Leonidas 57, Roberto 63
Czechoslovakia: Burkert, Burgr (c), Daucik, Kostalek, Boucek, Kopecky, Kreuz, Horak, Ludl, Senecky, Rulc
Goals: Kopecky 25
Referee: Capdeville (France)

Hungary, Sweden, Italy and Brazil qualified for semi-finals.

Semi-finals

At Paris' Parc des Princes stadium, **Hungary** showed the gulf in class between them and **Sweden** by annihilating the mediocre Scandinavians. Sweden had reached the semi-finals through good fortune in the draw and were not remotely in the same class as the other three teams, something which Hungary continued to show with relish throughout the game. It didn't start in such a way, however, Arne Nyberg incredibly putting the Swedes ahead with barely 30 seconds played. The Hungarians were stunned but they composed themselves and set about showing their absolute superiority. Gyula Zsengeller levelled things up after 19 minutes, Ferenc Sas added a second and then Zsengeller added his second and Hungary's third before half-time. In the second half, Hungary's domination was total as they utterly humiliated Sweden with their fantastic flowing football. The two goals they scored in the period, one for Gyorgy Sarosi and a third for Zsengeller, did no justice at all to the level of their domination. The Swedes would crawl away licking their wounds while the Hungarians would go into the final in top form and would be a match for anyone.

> **Only at the World Cup**
>
> Brazil foolishly rested striker Leonidas for their semi-final to keep him fresh for the final. Brazil proceeded to lose 2-1 to Italy. Nice one coach, a real masterstroke!

A potentially mouth-watering clash between **Italy** and **Brazil** took place that afternoon in Marseille. Sadly, the Brazilians were still exhausted from their gruelling two games against Czechoslovakia and, crucially, forward Leonidas was rested, supposedly to ensure he would be fit for the final. Without their inspirational centre forward, however, the South Americans lacked the ability to really challenge the world champions and surrendered the initiative to them. Italy took advantage to take the lead through Gino Colaussi, again a lively presence at outside left. Giuseppe Meazza was having another inspired game and he played in Silvio Piola, who was brought down by Domingos for a penalty. Despite his shorts falling down as he ran up to take the kick, Meazza still fired the spot kick past keeper Walter. Dealt such a double hammer blow, Brazil were left reeling and with little hope of a comeback. Romeu did score with three minutes remaining to set up a nervous finale but the Italians had few hiccups on the way. They would defend their trophy in the final, while Brazil had been the victims of the physicality of their quarter-final.

> **Only at the World Cup**
>
> Giuseppe Meazza's penalty against Brazil saw one of the most bizarre incidents of any World Cup. As he ran up to take the kick, the inside right's shorts fell down as the elastic snapped! Rather than stop, Meazza pulled up his shorts with one hand while shooting past keeper Walter, who was too busy laughing to attempt to save!

Semi-final results

Hungary 5-1 Sweden
16/06/38 – Paris (Parc des Princes)
Hungary: A Szabo, Koranyi, S Biro, Lazar, Turay, Szalay, Sas, Zsengeller, G Sarosi (c), Toldi, Titkos
Goals: Zsengeller 19, 39, 85, Sas 37, G Sarosi 65
Sweden: Abrahamsson, Eriksson, Kallgren, Almgren, Jacobsson, Svanstrom, Wetterstrom, Keller (c), H Andersson, Jonasson, Nyberg
Goals: Nyberg 1
Referee: Leclerq (France)

Italy 2-1 Brazil
16/06/38 – Marseille (Velodrome)
Italy: Olivieri, Foni, Rava, Serantoni, Andreolo, Locatelli, Biavati, Meazza (c), Piola, Ferrari, Colaussi
Goals: Colaussi 51, Meazza pen 60
Brazil: Walter, Domingos, Machado, Zeze Procopio, Martim Silveira (c), Afonsinho, Lopes, Luizinho, Peracio, Romeu, Patesko
Goals: Romeu 87
Referee: Wuthrich (Switzerland)

Hungary and Italy qualified for final, Sweden and Brazil to third-place play-off.

World Cup Great – Leonidas (Brazil)

Brazilian football is synonymous with gorgeous attacking play and extravagantly gifted forwards capable of producing the cheeky, unexpected and sublime on a regular basis. Probably the first player of this sort that Brazil ever produced was little centre forward Leonidas, the "Black Diamond".

Leonidas started his career as a 16-year-old at little Sao Cristovao, the same club where later another Brazilian striking legend, Ronaldo, would also make his bow. He lived something of a nomadic existence in his early years, successful wherever he went but rarely staying longer than a year. He enjoyed his first real taste of success at club level when he won the Rio de Janeiro state championship twice in successive years, first with Vasco de Gama and then with their local rivals Botafogo.

Around the same time, the young Leonidas was establishing himself in the Brazilian national team. Aged just 20, he did just enough to get himself into the starting line-up for Brazil's first-round clash with Spain in the 1934 World Cup. Despite losing 3-1, Leonidas announced his presence by scoring Brazil's only goal. A hero was born.

Following his exploits for Brazil and Botafogo, he transferred to Flamengo, the giants of the Rio scene, in 1936. Flamengo were notorious at the time, as too were the Brazilian national team, for racist selection policies but Leonidas' brilliant, exuberant performances cemented his place as the star of both teams. Few players played a bigger role in changing the racist nature of Brazilian football than Leonidas.

Leonidas' finest moments without a doubt came in the 1938 World Cup. It may have been relatively early in his career but the Second World War meant the striker would not have another chance on the big stage. Lucky, then, that he grabbed his opportunity firmly with both hands, starting off with a superb hat-trick against Poland and finishing up with seven goals in four matches as Brazil finished third. It might have been even more had coach Adhemar Pimenta not rested him for the semi-final with Italy, which Brazil then proceeded to lose. Nevertheless, he was one of the stars of the tournament and finished its top scorer.

Leonidas would leave the national team with a phenomenal record of 21 goals in just 19 caps, a superb haul even in the 1930s and 40s. At club level he joined Sao Paulo in 1942 and would remain there for the rest of his career, eventually retiring in 1950. He would briefly become manager of Sao Paulo before abandoning football for a quieter life. He died from Alzheimer's disease in 2004.

Leonidas was a prolific scorer of goals but it was the manner in which he scored them that was central to him becoming a fan favourite. He was one of the earliest pioneers of the bicycle kick, which started to enter the footballing psyche in the late 30s, while he also scored many goals with spectacular long range efforts. His cheeky, sometimes outrageous skills, all performed with a smile on his face, made him in many ways the prototype for so many other Brazilian greats who would follow him. Leonidas was the superstar Brazil needed to inspire the generations to come to turn the country into the world's premier footballing nation. For that, the country owes him a huge debt of gratitude.

Third-place Play-off

At the same time as the final was being played in Paris, Bordeaux played host to the third-place play-off between **Sweden** and **Brazil**. The South Americans, with Leonidas back in their team, were expected to win comfortably but Sweden surprised them by playing bright positive football early on and taking a two-goal lead, Sven Jonasson and Arne Nyberg on target, and it looked like they might earn themselves a measure of redemption for their thrashing at the hands of Hungary. However, Romeu's goal just before the break seemed to galvanise the Brazilians and they came out a different side in the second half. Leonidas took centre stage, firing home two goals to put Brazil ahead and himself out in front as the tournament's leading scorer with seven goals. Patesko then fired a penalty wastefully wide but it wasn't to matter. Sweden had nothing left in reply and Peracio finished it with a fourth Brazilian goal ten minutes from time. Brazil had won the bronze medal they richly deserved for their performances in the tournament. No doubt they will have wondered if the outcome could have been better still had Leonidas played in the semi-final against Italy.

Third-place Play-off result

Sweden 2-4 Brazil
19/06/38 – Bordeaux (Parc Lescure)
Sweden: Abrahamsson, Eriksson, Nilsson, Almgren, Linderholm, Svanstrom (c), Persson, A Andersson, H Andersson, Jonasson, Nyberg
Goals: Jonasson 28, Nyberg 38
Brazil: Batatais, Domingos, Machado, Zeze Procopio, Brandao, Afonsinho, Roberto, Romeu, Leonidas (c), Peracio, Patesko
Goals: Romeu 44, Leonidas 63, 74, Peracio 80
Referee: Langenus (Belgium)

Brazil claimed third place.

World Cup Final

Italy had the chance to defend their title at the Stade Olympique de Colombes in Paris, with **Hungary** their opposition. Four years earlier, the Italians had been nervy and desperately fortunate to beat Czechoslovakia. This time, however, perhaps helped by their experience or the absence of the pressure created by Mussolini watching over them, they were exceptional from start to finish. Brilliant captain and playmaker Giuseppe Meazza had his finest game of the tournament, pulling the strings delightfully and providing the ammunition for his darting team mates. It was a Meazza pass that helped put Italy in front just six minutes in. He fed Gino Colaussi, running in from the left and the winger fired powerfully past Antal Szabo. The Hungarians, though, were undeterred and hit back just two minutes later, the ball worked well to the onrushing Pal Titkos, who buried a ferocious shot from the left edge of the area. Italy didn't let this setback affect them, however, and were still utterly dominant. Their patient, incisive build-up play paid dividends soon after as they scored a fantastically constructed goal. A beautiful passing movement culminated in Meazza taking on the shattered Hungarian defence before neatly feeding Silvio Piola to drive powerfully home and restore the holders' lead. Ten minutes before the end of the first half it was 3-1, Meazza playing another gorgeously weighted pass into the run of Colaussi, again drifting in off his wing, and the forward ran on before rolling the ball effortlessly into the back of the net. It would take something very special for the Hungarians to respond to a performance like that after the break and predictably it proved beyond them. Nevertheless, they weren't about to go down without a fight and when, with 20 minutes remaining, Gyorgy Sarosi burst into the box to smash past Olivieri into the top corner, there briefly seemed like they might have the opportunity to rescue the game. However, it was not to be, the Italians scoring the fourth goal their brilliant performance deserved. Piola, exceptional in the game and the tournament, was the beneficiary of a delightful cut-back from Amedeo Biavati which he buried thunderously in the back of the net. The Italians were joyful as they celebrated a thoroughly deserved triumph, one that this time came much less tainted than that on home soil four years earlier. Given the biggest stage of all, they had emphatically proved just why they were world champions.

> **Only at the World Cup**
>
> There is no doubt the Italians were brilliant in their victory over Hungary but some have since suggested the Hungarians lost on purpose! The logic for this comes from a telegram sent to the Italians by Mussolini before the final which literally translated said: "Win or die." Hungary goalkeeper Antal Szabo would reference this after the match by saying: "I may have let in four goals but at least I saved their lives." However, the phrase "Vincere o morire" was frequently used to mean, "Give your all to try to win" and the likelihood the fascist government would murder a team so beneficial to their propaganda was minimal. Bet there were a few brown pairs of shorts going for laundry afterwards though!

World Cup Final result

Hungary 2-4 Italy
19/06/38 – Paris (Colombes)
Hungary: A Szabo, Polgar, S Biro, Szalay, Szucs, Lazar, Sas, Vincze, G Sarosi (c), Zsengeller, Titkos
Goals: Titkos 8, G Sarosi 70
Italy: Olivieri, Foni, Rava, Serantoni, Andreolo, Locatelli, Biavati, Meazza (c), Piola, Ferrari, Colaussi
Goals: Colaussi 6, 35, Piola 16, 82
Referee: Capdeville (France)

Italy won the 1938 World Cup.

Tournament awards

Golden Boot: Leonidas (Brazil) – 7 goals
(Runner-up: Gyula Zsengeller (Hungary) – 6)

Best Player: Giuseppe Meazza (Italy)

Best Goal: Silvio Piola (Italy) – A beautifully constructed and finished goal to kill off hopes of a Hungarian comeback late on in the final. Right winger Amedeo Biavati produced an exquisite cut-back and Piola smashed the ball first time with a thunderous drive past Antal Szabo.

Star XI:
Goalkeeper – Frantisek Planicka (Czechoslovakia)
Defenders – Domingos da Guia (Brazil), Pietro Rava (Italy)
Midfielders – Pietro Serantoni (Italy), Michele Andreolo (Italy), Ugo Locatelli (Italy)
Forwards – Gyula Zsengeller (Hungary), Giuseppe Meazza (Italy), Silvio Piola (Italy), Leonidas (Brazil), Gino Colaussi (Italy)

World Cup Great – Giuseppe Meazza (Italy)

Many of the stars of the 1930s have sadly been forgotten by many, existing merely as names on rotting team-sheets in archives out of sight and memory. For Italy's brilliant inside forward and key playmaker Giuseppe Meazza, however, his name has been immortalised as the official title of the San Siro stadium in Milan, the home of his beloved Internazionale as well as AC Milan, for whom Meazza also played in a glittering career.

Growing up without a father, Meazza was rejected by Milan as a teenager for his slight frame. However, their great rivals Inter snapped him up soon after and he soon became the heartbeat of their side. Playing originally as a centre forward, Meazza was a prolific goal scorer, notching an impressive 31 goals in his debut Serie A season despite still being in his teens. His goals and brilliant performances helped Inter win the league title in 1930 ahead of a fancied Juventus team. That same year, Meazza won his first international cap against Switzerland and marked the occasion by scoring twice.

By the time the 1934 World Cup in Italy had come around, Italy coach Vittorio Pozzo had converted Meazza into an inside forward in his renowned Metodo system. This involved Meazza dropping back into the midfield to make the play and set up chances from deep, also allowing him to take on defenders with his legendary dribbling runs. The move worked perfectly. Meazza was the star of the show, scoring twice and setting up countless more for his team mates as the Azzurri carried off the title on home soil.

Meazza also established himself as a phenomenal leader for club and country, his inspirational performances serving as a huge encouragement to his team mates. He was captain for Italy's defence of the world title in 1938. Now firmly established as the side's general, he and inside forward partner Giovanni Ferrari were the fulcrum on which Italy's challenge was built. Meazza may have only scored once but he was absolutely masterful in possession, providing countless assists for his team mates and giving a veritable masterclass in the final, laying on three of Italy's four goals for his team mates. He formed a particularly fruitful partnership with Juventus centre forward Silvio Piola, whose size and strength perfectly complimented Meazza's skill, passing and vision.

Meazza would continue delighting the Inter fans until 1940, when he signed for great rivals Milan. However, the legendary status he enjoyed at Inter was undiminished. Indeed, to this day many Inter fans still worship him and consider him their greatest ever player. After something of a nomadic existence in his later career, Meazza would eventually return to his beloved Inter for his final season, 1946-7, the Nerazzurri welcoming back their darling with open arms.

One of the game's first superstars, Meazza was unlike many of his contemporaries in that he enjoyed a high profile off the pitch as well as on it. Famous for his playboy lifestyle, he was one of the earliest players to receive personal sponsorship. It was not the only way he was ahead of his time. One of the very first midfield generals, there have been few better players throughout history in "the hole" than Meazza, even though he was one of the pioneers of the position. Blessed with astonishing vision and passing ability, the role suited him perfectly. Allied to this was his formidable goalscoring ability, which served him so well in his early career as a centre forward. Indeed, his record of 33 international goals, scored in just 53 games, is still the second highest ever by an Italian, with only Luigi Riva having surpassed him.

Meazza is still well known even today for his trademark runs. He was a master at dribbling, even at a time when the practice was infinitely more common than today, with close ball control and speed of movement and thought that eclipsed even the majority of Brazilian stars, with whom such qualities are normally associated. He scored a host of goals in his career by dribbling his way through the defence before rounding the keeper and rolling the ball into the empty net. Even today, goals scored in such a fashion are often likened to Meazza in Italy, just another way his name has been immortalised. Though Italy will always be thought of in footballing terms above all for its great defence, few countries have ever produced a forward or attacking midfielder with half the ability of Meazza, who surely, even to this day, remains Italy's greatest ever attacking player.

In the end, Italy had done enough to retain the title they had won four years earlier. This triumph, in contrast, was altogether less controversial, topped off by that masterclass in the final. The Italians had shown the extent of their undoubted quality. Players like Meazza and Piola had proven themselves among the very best in the world and they had thoroughly deserved to win.

Hungary, their opponents in the final, had shown they were constantly improving at international level. They had faced some modest opponents but their performances had easily been worthy of the final. However, Brazil were generally considered to have been Italy's closest challengers in the tournament. Whether the Brazilians could have beaten the champions had brilliant centre forward Leonidas played is open to debate but they had proven that South American teams could be competitive in Europe. However, few would wish to remember the appalling nature of their clash with Czechoslovakia. The poor Czechs, who again had shown their quality in the tournament, had ultimately only gone out because of serious injuries to their best players. They had been hopelessly unlucky.

Preparations were made for the next competition, pencilled in for 1942. However, all those plans were soon made meaningless by the outbreak of the Second World War, the seemingly inevitable arrival of which had cast a sombre mood over the 1938 tournament. The war and its aftermath instantly sidelined football, with the competitions of 1942 and 1946 unable to take place. It would not be for 12 years until the world, finally at peace again and beginning to recover from the tragedy of the millions killed in the awful carnage, could once again join together in the mutual appreciation and celebration of football and rejoice in the unity that sport can bring.

> **Only at the World Cup**
>
> While war raged, stopping the World Cup being held for 12 years, Italian sports officials removed the Jules Rimet Trophy from storage in a Rome bank and gave it to their secretary, Dr Otto Barassi, who hid it in a shoebox under his bed to avoid discovery!

1950: Brazil

Qualification

> **Only at the World Cup**
>
> Although Axis powers Germany and Japan were banned, strangely their ally Italy was allowed to take part. Of course it was just coincidence they were champions and knew where the trophy was hidden…

34 Entrants.
Italy qualified as holders.
Brazil qualified as hosts.

Group 1

Northern Ireland 2-8 Scotland, Wales 1-4 England, Scotland 2-0 Wales, England 9-2 Northern Ireland, Wales 0-0 Northern Ireland, Scotland 0-1 England

	Pld	W	D	L	GF	GA	Pts
England	3	3	0	0	14	3	6
Scotland	3	2	0	1	10	3	4
Wales	3	0	1	2	1	6	1
Northern Ireland	3	0	1	2	4	17	1

England and **Scotland** qualified. However, Scotland withdrew. France were invited to replace them but declined.

Group 2

Turkey v Syria: 7-0, Syria withdrew before return.
Austria v Turkey: Austria withdrew.

Turkey qualified but later withdrew. Portugal were invited to replace them but declined after seeing their itinerary.

> **Only at the World Cup**
>
> Scotland held by their assertion before the tournament that they would only compete if they won the Home Nations Championship. France were initially keen to replace them but declined when they saw the distance they would have to travel between matches. Added to Turkey's withdrawal and Portugal's refusal to replace them, the tournament was already left two teams short.

Group 3

Yugoslavia v Israel: 6-0, 5-2 (agg. 11-2)
Yugoslavia v France: 1-1, 1-1 (agg. 2-2)
Play-off in Italy: Yugoslavia 3-2 France (aet)

Yugoslavia qualified. France were later offered a place but declined.

Group 4

Switzerland v Luxembourg: 5-2, 3-2 (agg. 8-4)
Belgium v Switzerland: Belgium withdrew.

Switzerland qualified.

Group 5

Sweden 3-1 Ireland, Ireland 3-0 Finland, Finland 1-1 Ireland, Ireland 1-3 Sweden
Finland withdrew and their remaining matches were cancelled.

Sweden qualified. FIFA later contacted Ireland to ask if they would be interested in entering the competition in the event of a vacancy but they declined.

Group 6

Spain v Portugal: 5-1, 2-2 (agg. 7-3)

Spain qualified. Portugal were later invited to replace Turkey but declined.

Group 7

Argentina withdrew after an argument with the Brazilian federation.

Bolivia and **Chile** qualified.

Group 8

Ecuador and Peru withdrew.

Paraguay and **Uruguay** qualified.

Group 9 (in Mexico)

USA 0-6 Mexico, Mexico 2-0 Cuba, Cuba 1-1 USA, Mexico 6-2 USA, USA 5-2 Cuba, Cuba 0-3 Mexico

	Pld	W	D	L	GF	GA	Pts
Mexico	4	4	0	0	17	2	8
USA	4	1	1	2	8	15	3
Cuba	4	0	1	3	3	11	1

Mexico and **USA** qualified.

Group 10

Burma, Indonesia and Philippines withdrew.

India qualified but later withdrew also because of an argument with FIFA.

> **Only at the World Cup**
>
> The 1950 tournament ended up being three teams short after India also withdrew because FIFA would not allow them to play barefoot!

The Contenders

Bolivia	Sweden
Brazil	Switzerland
Chile	Uruguay
England	USA
Italy	Yugoslavia
Mexico	India (withdrawn)
Paraguay	Scotland (withdrawn)
Spain	Turkey (withdrawn)

So finally, after 12 years of war, hardship and suffering, the world could join together and celebrate the joy of an international football tournament once more. Given much of Europe lay strewn in ruins, it was hardly surprising that the World Cup returned to South America, with Brazil – who had been the leading contenders to host the cancelled 1942 competition ahead of Nazi Germany – the only country who had bid for it. The previous three tournaments had all been held in relatively small countries so FIFA had a massive task on their hands ensuring travel across Brazil's vast expanse was kept to a minimum. This, however, they failed spectacularly, opting against basing each group in a certain area, as would frequently be done in later World Cups also hosted in large countries. This meant travel fatigue would combine with factors such as climate and altitude to further hinder visiting teams.

As with the previous tournament held in South America, in 1930, a meagre 13 teams would compete thanks to several withdrawals and FIFA's chaotic organisation hardly encouraging others to step in to replace them. Despite these withdrawals, FIFA made another poor decision by not rearranging the groups, leaving two pools of four, one of three and, incredibly, one of just two teams, which would surely give the winner a huge advantage as they would be far fresher for the later stages of the tournament.

Many of Europe's best teams would be absent, still recovering from the horrors of the war which had torn their continent apart. Germany, defeated by the Allies, would be banned from this tournament as part of their punishment, while several other top European teams, amongst them Austria, Hungary, Czechoslovakia and the USSR, opted not to take part. However, for the first time the British teams, back with FIFA, had taken part, with England being their sole representative due to Scotland's withdrawal. Nevertheless, the weakening of the European field meant that the South American teams would be heavily favoured on their own continent, even with one of their finest, Argentina, declining to attend.

Most heavily fancied of all were the hosts **Brazil**, an exceptionally talented team boosted by home advantage, fanatical support and playing all their games at the nearby cities of Rio de Janeiro and Sao Paulo, avoiding the hours of travelling the other sides would experience. They boasted an exceptional forward line of Zizinho, Ademir and Jair, all supremely talented players. Without question they would be the team to beat. Joining them in Group One would be **Yugoslavia**, who Brazil would not remember fondly after the Europeans pipped them to the semi-finals in 1930. Olympic silver medallists in London in 1948, they too came with a massively talented squad, including outstanding schemer Rajko Mitic and deadly striker Stjepan Bobek. They would be Brazil's most dangerous first-round opponents. **Switzerland** would also be competing in the group. They would still have veteran striker Alfred Bickel, a young star of the 1938 tournament, in their side and he would be aided in the goalscoring department by the likes of Charles Antenen and Jacques Fatton, both dangerous players. However, they could well be porous at the back, as their key defender, former Chelsea left-back Willi Steffen, was struggling with his fitness. Completing the group were **Mexico**, who had qualified convincingly by thrashing the USA and Cuba. However, against higher quality opponents they were likely to struggle. Young keeper Antonio Carbajal would surely be a busy man.

In Group Two, **England**, competing in their first World Cup, would be the most fancied team. The creators of the game still terrified opponents, who held them in awe. They boasted a fine team, with many wartime legends still present. Among them were the famous wing pairing of Stanley Matthews and Tom Finney, as well as fearsome forwards Jackie Milburn, Stan Mortensen and Wilf Mannion, a frontline that would strike fear into anyone. They would be tight at the back too, with legendary centre half or wing half Billy Wright the centrepiece and right-back Alf Ramsey a capable assistant. Their closest challengers were expected to be **Spain**, a fine side in their own right, boasting a formidable attacking trio of Estanislao Basora, Agustin Gainza and the prolific centre forward Zarra. They would put up a strong fight. **Chile** too would come with a chance. George Robledo, a team mate of Milburn's at Newcastle United, would lead their line, while keeper Sergio Livingstone would use his athleticism to keep the score down at the other end. Still, they were not anywhere near the same league as England or Spain. The **USA** were expected to be the group's whipping boys. Twice thrashed by Mexico, conceding 12 goals in their two matches against them, it didn't bode well for their chances against two European heavyweights.

Reigning champions **Italy** were drawn in Group Three but they would have next to no chance of defending their title. Their all-conquering Torino side, who had cleaned up domestic honours for four successive seasons and provided the heartbeat of the national team, including star playmaker Valentino Mazzola, had tragically all been killed the previous year in the Superga air disaster. Deprived of their best players, there appeared little hope of them retaining the trophy but at least they had still come, even though, unsurprisingly, they chose not to fly. Italy's weakness in the group seemed to open the door to the **Sweden** side coached by legendary Yorkshireman George Raynor. They had been brilliant in winning the Olympic title two years earlier but that side had been decimated as key attacking trio Gunnar Nordahl, Gunnar Gren and Nils Liedholm had all gone to ply their trade with AC Milan and the Swedish FA had a policy of not picking professionals. Still, in veteran skipper Erik Nilsson, a youngster at the 1938 tournament, dominant centre half Knut Nordahl and gifted young inside forward Lennart Skoglund they had quality players. India's withdrawal left **Paraguay** as the only other team in the group. They had finished second in the South American Championships in 1949 but with star forward Arsenio Erico now retired and their professional players absent, there looked little hope of their inexperienced and entirely home-based team making much of an impact.

The withdrawals of Turkey and Scotland meant just two teams contested Group Four. **Uruguay** were by far the more fancied of the two. They would be back for the first time since winning the World Cup on home soil back in 1930 and again boasted a quality side, bossed by inspirational captain and centre half Obdulio Varela and also featuring the supreme talents of inside forward Juan Schiaffino and centre forward Oscar Omar Miguez. They would also implement coach Juan Lopez's revolutionary new system, which placed greater emphasis on defence. In modern-day terms, it was effectively a change from the 2-3-5, 2-3-2-3 or 3-2-5 played by most teams at the time to something more akin to a modern-day 4-3-3, with the full-backs playing more as centre-backs, wing halves Schubert Gambetta and Victor Rodriguez Andrade, both equally adept on either side, playing on the flanks of the defence like the full-backs of today, centre half Varela moving up to support the inside forwards, who dropped deeper to work as midfield schemers, leaving the wingers to push up and support centre forward Miguez. With greater security at the back, Uruguay would be extremely tough to beat, particularly for the minnows of **Bolivia**, their luckless first-round opponents. One of the weakest South American teams, they could well be on the end of a convincing hiding against the darting Uruguayans.

Debutants: England

The Draw

Group 1
Brazil
Mexico
Switzerland
Yugoslavia

Group 2
Chile
England
Spain
USA

Group 3
Italy
Paraguay
Sweden
(India)

Group 4
Bolivia
Uruguay
(Scotland)
(Turkey)

Venues:
Rio de Janeiro, Belo Horizonte, Curitiba, Porto Alegre, Recife, Sao Paulo

---

Stat Attack

The 1950 tournament was the first World Cup where players wore numbers on the back of their shirts. However, at this stage players could change numbers with each match rather than keeping one all tournament.

The Tournament – 24 June-16 July

Group Stage – First series

Brazil opened the tournament in front of their adoring fans at the newly built Maracana stadium in Rio de Janeiro, given the relatively simple task of dispensing of **Mexico**. This they achieved without fuss, even being able to leave key creator Zizinho out of their side and still win at a canter. Deadly striker Ademir's pace, power and lethal finishing proved altogether too good for the Central Americans and he opened the scoring to rapturous acclaim half an hour in. The Brazilians never really had to get out of second gear and coasted along until midway through the second half, when they suddenly buried the Mexicans under an avalanche of goals. Tricky schemer Jair scored Brazil's second before Baltazar also found the target with a powerful header, very much the striker's forte, and Ademir got his second, resulting in a final score of 4-0. Brazil had not played their best football but it hadn't mattered as they had won comfortably and convincingly. They would save themselves for greater challenges ahead.

In Group Two, **England** played their first ever World Cup match the next day against **Chile**, also in the grand theatre of the Maracana. Leaving out Stanley Matthews and Jackie Milburn seemed to suggest England predicted an easy victory and so it proved. Big centre forward Stan Mortensen powered in an unstoppable header midway through the first half and there never looked much danger of a Chilean comeback. England were afforded plenty of time on the ball and didn't over-exert themselves in the unfamiliar conditions, adding some breathing space through a Wilf Mannion goal but hardly busting a gut to increase their lead. In the end, it proved a gentle and comfortable opener for England to ease themselves into World Cup football.

> **Stat Attack**
>
> Blackpool striker Stan Mortensen scored England's first ever World Cup goal in the win over Chile.

Elsewhere in the group, the unfancied **USA** came close to pulling off a shock win over **Spain** in Curitiba. John Souza powered them in front early on, exploiting the nerves of keeper Ignacio Eizaguirre to give them a surprise lead. Incredibly, through desperate defending, wasteful Spanish shooting and considerable luck, they were still 1-0 up going into the final 15 minutes. However, at last Spain found their scoring touch, speedy outside right Estanislao Basora netting twice in quick succession to turn the tie on its head. The US, stunned, succumbed to a further sucker punch from Zarra, who thundered a late header home for 3-1. However, Spain had been left sweating till the end and the Americans had given a far better account of themselves than anyone had expected, especially after their atrocious displays in qualification.

Meanwhile in Sao Paulo, **Italy**'s hopes of defending their trophy were all but ended as they succumbed to the narrowest of defeats at the hands of **Sweden** in Group Three's opening game. It all started so well for the beleaguered champions, skipper Riccardo Carapellese firing them in front after just seven minutes. However, their hopes were to be short lived, centre forward Hasse Jeppson and wing half Sunne Andersson scoring in quick succession. Jeppson added a third midway through the second half and it looked like it was all over. The Italians were not about to go down without a fight, however, Ermes Muccinelli pulling it back to 3-2 with 15 minutes to play. With the Swedes hanging on, Carapellese, a menace throughout, thought he'd levelled things up with seconds remaining but his ferocious shot came back off the crossbar. Defeat meant Italy's World Cup challenge was already all but over.

Later that day, **Yugoslavia** got their tournament underway against **Switzerland** in Belo Horizonte. With Rajko Mitic pulling the strings brilliantly, the Yugoslavs were dominant throughout but surprisingly it took an hour for them to put themselves on the scoresheet through centre forward Kosta Tomasevic. However, once the goal did arrive, two more followed in quick succession, Tomasevic adding his second before Tihomir Ognjanov also got himself on the scoresheet late on. Ending 3-0, the scoreline didn't do justice to the extent of Yugoslavia's domination or the brilliance of Mitic, so unlucky not to score himself in an inspired performance.

> ### Stat Attack
>
> Swiss forward Alfred Bickel set a record against Yugoslavia for longest gap between World Cup appearances, his previous start coming in the quarter-final defeat to Hungary in 1938. Bickel and Sweden defender Erik Nilsson were the only two players to compete in World Cups before and after the Second World War.

Group Stage – Second series

Back in Group One, **Brazil**, showing several changes in their team after coach Flavio Costa bowed to external pressures on his selection, were unable to find their form and could only manage a 2-2 draw with **Switzerland**, much to the shock and horror of their hordes of fans in Sao Paulo. It started well enough, one of the new arrivals, Alfredo, putting the hosts ahead just three minutes in. It proved a false dawn, however, World Cup veteran Alfred Bickel swinging in a cross for the roaming Jacques Fatton to firmly ram home. Brazil were unperturbed, however, and big centre forward Baltazar connected with a header to restore their lead before half-time. However, despite applying considerable pressure on the Swiss goal, another goal remained beyond the Brazilians. In the absence of key creators Zizinho and Jair, Ademir and Baltazar struggled to create chances for themselves up front and they were made to pay for their failure to kill the game when Fatton scored a second totally against the run of play with just two minutes remaining. Brazil had been halted and now were in danger of missing out on progressing.

Yugoslavia capitalised on Brazil's hiccup against Switzerland by inflicting another heavy defeat on **Mexico** in Porto Alegre to take control of the group. The Yugoslavs were remarkably unaffected by their marathon trip down from Belo Horizonte, well north of Rio, to Porto Alegre in the country's far south and turned out another impressive performance, with the outstanding Mitic again to the fore. Croat hitman Stjepan Bobek set them on their way after 20 minutes and they never looked back, Zeljko Cajkovski, whose older brother Zlatko was playing at right half, scoring twice to put the Europeans in total control. Tomasevic put some gloss on the scoreline with a fourth ten minutes from time before Hector Ortiz at least gave the Mexicans some small consolation with a late penalty. However, it was most certainly Yugoslavia's day and they would need just a draw with Brazil in their final game to progress ahead of the hosts.

In the wide-open spaces of the Maracana, **Spain** enjoyed a comfortable victory over **Chile** without any of the nerves they had shown against the USA. The deadly duo of Basora and Zarra both scored in the first half hour and Chile never looked like staging a comeback, unimpressive just as they had been against England. Spain could afford to relax and not tire themselves out ahead of their crunch meeting with England, which would likely decide the winner of the group. Chile, after two successive defeats, were out with a game to spare.

Meanwhile, in Group Three, Italy were eliminated without even playing, since the point **Sweden** gained in drawing with **Paraguay** in Curitiba was enough to ensure they could not top the group. The Scandinavians were widely expected to beat the limited South Americans with ease and for half an hour it seemed that way after Stig Sundqvist and impressive midfield general Karl-Erik Palmer but them 2-0 up. However, Atilio Lopez pulled a goal back minutes later and the Paraguayans refused to give up,

> ### Stat Attack
>
> Italy held the World Cup for an incredible 16 successive years between 1934 and 1950, a record that will surely never be broken.

pouring forward whenever possible to mount attacks on Karl Svensson in the Swedish goal. With time running out, Cesar Lopez Fretes struck to bring it back to 2-2 and earn Paraguay an unlikely draw. Still, the result looked like securing qualification for Sweden, while Italy's hopes of a third successive World Cup triumph were over. Finally, the Jules Rimet Trophy would be going elsewhere.

The 29th of June 1950 and Belo Horizonte in Brazil have gone down in infamy in the annals of English football as the time and place where **England**'s aura of invincibility in global football was finally broken as they fell to one of the biggest shocks in World Cup history, astonishingly beaten by the **USA**. Their hammering at the hands of Hungary three years later is generally identified as the end of England's tenure at the top of world football but this result was far more shocking and unexpected. England were widely expected to make changes after failing to impress against Chile but Matthews and Milburn were again left out as Walter Winterbottom chose to keep the same 11 players. England tore out of the blocks and could have scored a dozen goals in the first half, twice hitting the post as goalkeeper Frank Borghi did brilliantly to deny Tom Finney and the ever-dangerous Stan Mortensen. Then, in the 38th minutes, the US sensationally took the lead. Walter Bahr's cross was met by a headlong dive from Haitian-born forward Joe Gaetjens, who just made contact with his header to take the ball beyond English keeper Bert Williams. The crowd, firmly backing the underdogs, erupted, but England were unshaken. They launched an all-out assault on the US goal for the duration of the second half but the brilliance of Borghi and the wastefulness of the England forwards saw no further score. Shockingly, the USA, who had been thought of almost as a joke team before the start of the tournament, had beaten one of the giants of world football. They had definitely been incredibly lucky but their whole-hearted performance against Spain proved this was no fluke. For England there was only despair and humiliation. Middlesbrough inside forward Wilf Mannion summed up the feelings of the England camp after the game, exclaiming: "Bloody ridiculous! Can't we play them again tomorrow?" Sadly for Mannion and England, they could not and their chances of progression had been severely damaged.

> **Only at the World Cup**
>
> The USA's incredible 1-0 win over England sent shockwaves through world football and remains one of the greatest upsets of all time. Indeed, it was so shocking that many in England thought the scoreline was a misprint and thought England had won 10-1! No, sorry guys, you'd better get used to World Cup failure!

Group Stage – Third series

In Rio, **Brazil** and **Yugoslavia** faced each other for a place in the final round, the Europeans knowing that a draw would be enough to see them through. The Brazilians, knowing they were firmly up against the ropes, recalled their star forwards Zizinho and Jair, who would do battle with Yugoslavia's chief creator, Rajko Mitic. However, Mitic would take centre stage in the build-up to the game, injuring his head minutes before kick-off and forcing the Yugoslavs to begin the game with just ten men. The Brazilians instantly made their man advantage count, Ademir rising to head past Srdjan Mrkusic for 1-0. Mitic did return soon after but, no doubt shaken from his blow, he was short of the star of

> **Only at the World Cup**
>
> Yugoslavia were dealt a blow against Brazil before the start of the game when Rajko Mitic banged his head on a metal girder on his way out of the tunnel and missed the start of the match while it was bandaged up. When he did get on, he was so dazed he was unaware Ademir had already put Brazil ahead until his team mates told him at half-time!

the opening two games. Still, he made a big difference to Yugoslavia and the side gave a much-improved performance after his return. Nevertheless, it wasn't enough to breach Barbosa's goal and Brazil made sure of victory when the impressive Bauer picked out Zizinho and the darling of the home side slotted home with aplomb. Brazil had done enough, beating a very fine side to book their place in the final round. With their population passionately and loudly behind them, they would certainly take some stopping.

England, coming off the back of their aberration against the USA, had to beat **Spain** at the Maracana to have any hope of progressing. Matthews and Milburn were both recalled and England gave a much-improved performance. They had Spain on the back foot for the majority of the game but Antonio Ramallets, selected ahead of Eizaguirre in goal, produced a string of impressive saves. However, he was powerless to keep out a bullet header from Milburn but referee Galeati incorrectly ruled the effort out for offside. Deflated, England fell to defeat when Agustin Gainza headed down a centre and the lurking Zarra stabbed home from close in. It was the end of a nightmare debut World Cup for England, while for Spain there was joy and a place in the final round.

Meanwhile, already-eliminated **Italy** took on **Paraguay**, who could theoretically still progress with victory in Sao Paulo. The Italians, with nothing to play for, were still comfortably the better side against uninspired opponents. They won easily 2-0, Riccardo Carapellese and Egisto Pandolfini supplying the goals for a disappointed team who played at half-pace all game. Still, given the loss of the core players of their team, they had at least gone down fighting and signed off with a victory. For Paraguay, their slim hopes of progressing evaporated with defeat.

In Porto Alegre, two more teams assured of elimination, **Mexico** and **Switzerland** did battle for pride. After a delayed start due to a colour clash between the teams, the action eventually got underway with the Swiss scoring twice early on, Rene Bader and Jean Tamini putting them two goals to the good by half-time. The Europeans held the lead comfortably to the end to claim the win they deserved but the Mexicans did at least leave the tournament with one more goal to their name, experienced striker Horacio Casarin bagging the consolation. Mexico's second World Cup appearance, however, had been no more successful than their first. At least they could take consolation that their conquerors Switzerland would also be on the plane home despite their victory.

> **Only at the World Cup**
>
> Mexico's clash with Switzerland was postponed by 25 minutes after both teams arrived with the same colour strip! Eventually, replacements were found and the match could get underway.

Back in Group Two, **Chile** and the **USA** also played out a meaningless game in Recife, since Spain's earlier victory meant the Americans' already slim hopes of reaching the final round were utterly extinguished. Anyway, they had played their hand against Spain and England and now they had nothing left in the tank. The Chileans, hitherto a disappointment, used the opportunity to rebuild their damaged reputation, rampaging to a dominant 5-2 victory. George Robledo and Fernando Riera put Chile two goals up at the break but the USA struck back to level soon after, Frank Wallace pulling one back and John Souza levelling from the spot. Still, the South Americans were to have their victory, running riot late on with Atilio Cremaschi bagging two goals and Andres Prieto also scoring. Their victory was of little use, however, as they were already out after defeats in their first two games.

In Belo Horizonte, as the other three groups were concluding their full cycle of matches, the only game in Group Four was also getting underway. As expected, **Bolivia** were no match at all for the pace and skill of **Uruguay**, who demolished them 8-0, scoring four times in each half. Uruguay tore out of the blocks

> **Only at the World Cup**
>
> FIFA's organisation had scandalously allowed Bolivia and Uruguay to contest Group Four on their own! This gave the victors, Uruguay, a huge advantage, as they would be far less tired than the other teams.

in the hope of killing off Bolivian hopes early and they achieved it. Oscar Miguez, Ernesto Vidal and Juan Schiaffino all scored in the first 20 minutes or so and when Miguez added a fourth before half-time, it was already all over. Bolivia fell apart in the second half and their opponents ran riot. Miguez quickly completed his hat-trick and Schiaffino doubled his personal tally before the last components of the forward line, attacking midfielder Julio Perez and little winger Alcides Ghiggia, also got in on the act late on. Uruguay were through without breaking sweat and also, crucially, without any of the travel fatigue of their opponents. They would be by far the freshest side in the final round.

First Round results

Group 1

Brazil 4-0 Mexico
24/06/50 – Rio de Janeiro (Maracana)
Brazil: Barbosa, Augusto (c), Juvenal, Bigode, Ely, Danilo, Maneca, Ademir, Baltazar, Jair, Friaca
Goals: Ademir 30, 79, Jair 65, Baltazar 71
Mexico: Carbajal, Zetter, Montemajor (c), Ruiz, Ochoa, Roca, Septien, Ortiz, Casarin, Perez, Velazquez
Referee: Reader (England)

Yugoslavia 3-0 Switzerland
25/06/50 – Belo Horizonte (Sete de Setembro)
Yugoslavia: Mrkusic, Horvat, Stankovic, Zlatko Cajkovski, Jovanovic, Djajic, Ognjanov, Mitic (c), Tomasevic, Bobek, Vukas
Goals: Tomasevic 60, 70, Ognjanov 75
Switzerland: Stuber, Neury, Bocquet, Lusenti, Eggimann, Quinche, Bickel (c), Antenen, Tamini, Bader, Fatton
Referee: Galeati (Italy)

Brazil 2-2 Switzerland
28/06/50 – Sao Paulo (Pacaembu)
Brazil: Barbosa, Augusto (c), Juvenal, Bauer, Rui, Noronha, Maneca, Ademir, Baltazar, Alfredo, Friaca
Goals: Alfredo 3, Baltazar 32
Switzerland: Stuber, Neury, Bocquet, Lusenti, Eggimann, Quinche, Bickel (c), Friedlander, Tamini, Bader, Fatton
Goals: Fatton 17, 88
Referee: Azon (Spain)

Yugoslavia 4-1 Mexico
28/06/50 – Porto Alegre (Estadio do Eucaliptos)
Yugoslavia: Mrkusic, Horvat (c), Stankovic, Zlatko Cajkovski, Jovanovic, Djajic, Mihajlovic, Mitic, Tomasevic, Bobek, Zeljko Cajkovski
Goals: Bobek 19, Zeljko Cajkovski 22, 62, Tomasevic 81
Mexico: Carbajal, Gutierrez, Gomez, Ruiz, Ochoa, Flores, Naranjo, Ortiz, Casarin (c), Perez, Velazquez
Goals: Ortiz pen 89
Referee: Leafe (England)

Brazil 2-0 Yugoslavia
01/07/50 – Rio de Janeiro (Maracana)
Brazil: Barbosa, Augusto (c), Juvenal, Bigode, Bauer, Danilo, Maneca, Zizinho, Ademir, Jair, Chico
Goals: Ademir 4, Zizinho 69
Yugoslavia: Mrkusic, Horvat, Stankovic, Zlatko Cajkovski (c), Jovanovic, Djajic, Vukas, Mitic, Tomasevic, Bobek, Zeljko Cajkovski
Referee: Griffiths (Wales)

Switzerland 2-1 Mexico
02/07/50 – Porto Alegre (Estadio do Eucaliptos)
Switzerland: Hug, Neury, Bocquet (c), Lusenti, Eggimann, Quinche, Antenen, Friedlander, Tamini, Bader, Fatton
Goals: Bader 10, Tamini 37
Mexico: Carbajal, Gutierrez, Gomez, Ochoa, Roca, Flores, Naranjo, Ortiz, Casarin (c), Borbolla, Velazquez
Goals: Casarin 89
Referee: Eklind (Sweden)

	Pld	W	D	L	GF	GA	Pts
Brazil	3	2	1	0	8	2	5
Yugoslavia	3	2	0	1	7	3	4
Switzerland	3	1	1	1	4	6	3
Mexico	3	0	0	3	2	10	0

Brazil qualified for final pool.

Group 2

England 2-0 Chile
25/06/50 – Rio de Janeiro (Maracana)
England: Williams, Ramsey, Aston, Wright (c), Hughes, Dickinson, Finney, Mortensen, Bentley, Mannion, Mullen
Goals: Mortensen 27, Mannion 51
Chile: Livingstone (c), Farias, Roldan, Alvarez, Busquet, Carvalho, Mayanes, Cremaschi, Robledo, Munoz, Diaz
Referee: Van der Meer (Holland)

Spain 3-1 USA
25/06/50 – Curitiba (Vila Capanema)
Spain: Eizaguirre (c), Alonso, Antunez, J Gonzalvo, M Gonzalvo, Puchades, Basora, Hernandez, Zarra, Igoa, Gainza
Goals: Basora 75, 78, Zarra 85
USA: Borghi, Keough (c), Maca, McIlvenny, Colombo, Bahr, Craddock, J Souza, Gaetjens, Pariani, Valentini
Goals: J Souza 17
Referee: Viana (Brazil)

Spain 2-0 Chile
29/06/50 – Rio de Janeiro (Maracana)
Spain: Ramallets, Alonso, Parra, J Gonzalvo, M Gonzalvo, Puchades, Basora, Panizo, Zarra, Igoa, Gainza (c)
Goals: Basora 17, Zarra 30
Chile: Livingstone (c), Farias, Roldan, Alvarez, Busquet, Carvalho, Prieto, Cremaschi, Robledo, Munoz, Diaz
Referee: Malcher (Brazil)

USA 1-0 England
29/06/50 – Belo Horizonte (Sete de Setembro)
USA: Borghi, Keough, Maca, McIlvenny (c), Colombo, Bahr, Wallace, J Souza, Gaetjens, Pariani, E Souza
Goals: Gaetjens 38
England: Williams, Ramsey, Aston, Wright (c), Hughes, Dickinson, Finney, Mortensen, Bentley, Mannion, Mullen
Referee: Dattilo (Italy)

Spain 1-0 England
02/07/50 – Rio de Janeiro (Maracana)
Spain: Ramallets, Alonso, Parra, J Gonzalvo, M Gonzalvo, Puchades, Basora, Panizo, Zarra, Igoa, Gainza (c)
Goals: Zarra 48
England: Williams, Ramsey, Eckersley, Wright (c), Hughes, Dickinson, Matthews, Mortensen, Milburn, Baily, Finney
Referee: Galeati (Italy)

Chile 5-2 USA
02/07/50 – Recife (Ilha do Retiro)
Chile: Livingstone (c), Farias, Machuca, Alvarez, Busquet, Rojas, Prieto, Cremaschi, Robledo, Riera, Ibanez
Goals: Robledo 16, Riera 32, Cremaschi 54, 82, Prieto 60
USA: Borghi, Keough, Maca, McIlvenny, Colombo, Bahr (c), Wallace, J Souza, Gaetjens, Pariani, E Souza
Goals: Wallace 47, J Souza pen 48
Referee: Gardelli (Brazil)

	Pld	W	D	L	GF	GA	Pts
Spain	3	3	0	0	6	1	6
England	3	1	0	2	2	2	2
Chile	3	1	0	2	5	6	2
USA	3	1	0	2	4	8	2

Spain qualified for final pool.

Group 3

Sweden 3-2 Italy
25/06/50 – Sao Paulo (Pacaembu)
Sweden: K Svensson, Samuelsson, E Nilsson (c), Andersson, K Nordahl, Gard, Sundqvist, Palmer, Jeppson, Skoglund, S Nilsson
Goals: Jeppson 25, 68, Andersson 33
Italy: Sentimenti, Giovannini, Furiassi, Annovazzi, Parola, Magli, Muccinelli, Boniperti, Cappello, Campatelli, Carapellese (c)
Goals: Carapellese 7, Muccinelli 75
Referee: Lutz (Switzerland)

Sweden 2-2 Paraguay
29/06/50 – Curitiba (Vila Capanema)
Sweden: K Svensson, Samuelsson, E Nilsson (c), Andersson, K Nordahl, Gard, Sundqvist, Palmer, Jeppson, Skoglund, Jonsson
Goals: Sundqvist 24, Palmer 26
Paraguay: Vargas, Gonzalito, Cespedes, Gavilan, Leguizamon, Cantero, E Avalos, A Lopez, Jara Saguier, Lopez Fretes (c), Unzaim
Goals: A Lopez 32, Lopez Fretes 89
Referee: Mitchell (Scotland)

Italy 2-0 Paraguay
02/07/50 – Sao Paulo (Pacaembu)
Italy: Moro, Blason, Furiassi, Fattori, Remondini, Mari, Muccinelli, Pandolfini, Cappello, Amadei, Carapellese (c)
Goals: Carapellese 12, Pandolfini 62
Paraguay: Vargas, Gonzalito, Cespedes, Gavilan, Leguizamon, Cantero, E Avalos, A Lopez, Jara Saguier, Lopez Fretes (c), Unzaim
Referee: Ellis (England)

	Pld	W	D	L	GF	GA	Pts
Sweden	2	1	1	0	5	4	3
Italy	2	1	0	1	4	3	2
Paraguay	2	0	1	1	2	4	1

Sweden qualified for final pool.

Group 4

Uruguay 8-0 Bolivia
02/07/50 – Belo Horizonte (Sete de Setembro)
Uruguay: Maspoli, Andrade, M Gonzalez, Tejera, J Gonzalez, Perez, Varela (c), Schiaffino, Ghiggia, Miguez, Vidal
Goals: Miguez 14, 45, 56, Vidal 18, Schiaffino 23, 59, Perez 73, Ghiggia 83
Bolivia: E Gutierrez, Acha, Bustamante (c), Greco, Valencia, Ferrel, Algaranez, Ugarte, Capparelli, B Gutierrez, Maldonado
Referee: Reader (England)

	Pld	W	D	L	GF	GA	Pts
Uruguay	1	1	0	0	8	0	2
Bolivia	1	0	0	1	0	8	0

Uruguay qualified for final pool.

Final Pool – First series

A week after the end of the group stage, the four remaining sides reconvened in Rio and Sao Paulo, drawn together in one final round-robin group, the winner of which would be crowned world champion. There would be no separate final or third-place play-off. Brazil would be based in Rio, while the matches not featuring the hosts would take place in neighbouring Sao Paulo. **Brazil** got the action underway against **Sweden**, on paper the weakest of the four sides. Nevertheless, the Brazilians started nervously, the pressure of the occasion perhaps getting to them, and Sweden squandered some golden opportunities to take an early lead. It was to cost them dear. The Brazilians found their feet after quarter of an hour and instantly made it count, Ademir neatly putting them in front. Ademir now had the appetite for goals and soon doubled his tally and, as the Swedes reeled from this double blow, Chico compounded their misery by opening his account, 3-0 at half-time. That was nothing compared to the second half as Brazil gave an emphatic demonstration of their title credentials. They were bewitching all around the pitch, leaving the Scandinavians chasing shadows as the livewire Ademir ran riot and his cohorts darted around, pulling the defenders apart and providing ammunition for their in-form hitman. Within minutes of the start of the second period Ademir had completed his hat-trick and it wasn't long before he had a fourth to add to his ever-growing personal tally. Sune Andersson at least got the Swedes on the board with a penalty but it was a hollow victory and they were to concede twice more before the end. The brilliant winger Maneca capped his inspired performance with a well-taken goal before Chico got his second for a final score of 7-1, and against the reigning Olympic champions at that. Brazil had hit top form and the results were truly frightening.

It was an altogether different story at Sao Paulo, as **Uruguay** rescued a late draw against **Spain**. The Uruguayans, fresh from their annihilation of Bolivia and without the fatigue of three tough matches, took the lead early thanks to the tricky running of right winger Alcides Ghiggia, who deservedly got himself on the scoresheet. However, Spain had their own goalscoring star on the right wing, Estanislao Basora, and he fired home emphatically twice before half-time to give the Europeans an interval lead. The South Americans staged a second-half fightback but the heroics of Antonio Ramallets in the Spanish goal looked to have earned the Iberians a precious victory. However, Uruguay's inspirational captain and centre half Obdulio Varela had other ideas. As so often the rescuer of a lost cause for his side, it was the skipper, striding through the middle, who finally drove ferociously beyond the Herculean Ramallets to earn a share of the spoils. However, in the wake of Brazil's crushing victory, the draw didn't really do either side much good in their bid to finish above the hosts.

> **Stat Attack**
>
> The 1950 World Cup was the only one which finished without a final, though as it happened the last game featured the only two sides still capable of winning the tournament, making it a de facto final.

Final Pool – Second series

Four days after demolishing Sweden, **Brazil** proceeded to repeat the trick against **Spain** with a victory almost as emphatic. Many Brazilians had been nervous before the game about their team's chances against the deadly strike force of Basora and Zarra but in the end the Europeans proved no match at all for the brilliant pace, movement and precision passing and shooting the Brazilians exhibited. They settled their nerves with a goal after 15 minutes, the rampaging Ademir firing in off Spanish defender Jose Parra, who deflected the ball past keeper Ramallets. This proved the cue for another goalfest, with the darting Jair next to get in on the action, followed by Chico before the break. As against Sweden, Brazil saved their best until the second half, tearing the bewildered Spaniards apart with remarkable ease. Chico and Ademir both got their second goals of the game before the brilliant Zizinho, the catalyst for so much of Brazil's phenomenal play, deservedly got his name on the scoresheet too with Brazil's sixth goal, all in the space of barely an hour played. After that, Brazil relaxed and Spain were at least able to get a consolation goal, Silvestre Igoa on target. Nevertheless, with a final score of 6-1, Brazil had put down another convincing marker and looked all but unstoppable. Meanwhile, Spanish hopes of the title were over after this crushing defeat.

As against Spain, **Uruguay** struggled desperately against the well-organised **Sweden** side but eventually claimed the win they needed to prevent Brazil being crowned world champions with a game to spare. It all went wrong for them at the start, however, Karl-Erik Palmer, superb for Sweden throughout the tournament, putting the Scandinavians ahead with barely five minutes played. However, it would be the skill of the livewire Ghiggia that would earn the South Americans an equaliser before half-time, scoring for the third match in succession to tie the scores. Nevertheless, as Uruguay celebrated, Sweden went straight back up the other end to score through Stig Sundqvist and re-establish their lead. It looked as if Uruguay's hopes were about to be snuffed out but again they found unlikely salvation late on. This time it was centre forward Oscar Omar Miguez who was their hero, the darling of Penarol scoring twice in the space of eight minutes to change a 2-1 deficit into a 3-2 lead, an advantage they held to the finish. The result meant Uruguay could still win the title but only a win against all-conquering Brazil would suffice.

Final Pool – Third series

In what was effectively a third-place play-off in Sao Paulo, **Spain** and **Sweden** played for third place knowing nothing they could do would be enough to win the title. As a result, both sides made several changes and gave reserve players a run-out. Unsurprisingly, both teams started uncertainly but it was the Swedes who recovered better to all the changes. Stig Sundqvist and Bror Mellberg gave the Scandinavians a two-goal lead at the interval and Karl-Erik Palmer made sure of it with a third with ten minutes remaining. Still, the Spanish, unquestionably the better of the two sides throughout the tournament, at least got the consolation goal they

> **Stat Attack**
>
> The crowd that watched the final game at the Maracana is estimated as about 100 short of 200,000 people, by far the biggest crowd ever to watch a football match.

> **Stat Attack**
>
> Amazingly for such a strong footballing nation, Spain's fourth place in 1950 remained their best World Cup finish for 60 years.

deserved, the ever-dangerous Zarra scoring late on for a final score of 3-1. Sweden had claimed bronze.

And so to the final game of the tournament in the throbbing Maracana, where nigh on 200,000 people had gathered to witness what was surely a coronation for hosts **Brazil** as world champions. They had swept all before them in their previous matches and now only needed a draw against **Uruguay**, who had struggled desperately against the same opponents Brazil had put to the sword. There looked little hope of anything other than a Brazilian victory and that was certainly the way the Brazilian public saw it; indeed, they had already been celebrating as if Brazil had won days before and there was a sense of inevitability about proceedings. Not that Uruguay's ultra-confident skipper Obdulio Varela was intimidated, however, delivering a stirring and rousing speech to his troops before the game, instilling in them the same belief and will to win he had himself. They would be up for the contest and not merely passengers in a Brazilian procession as Sweden and Spain had been.

> **Only at the World Cup**
>
> The pressure got to Uruguay midfielder Julio Perez, who wet himself during the national anthems! "I am not ashamed of this", he later said. Classy!

The Uruguayans' determination paid dividends in the first half as they refused to be intimidated by the mammoth crowd and the dangerous attacking play of the Brazilians. Nevertheless, they were on the back foot throughout and keeper Roque Maspoli had to produce the performance of his life to deny the hosts, repeatedly keeping out the best efforts of Ademir, Zizinho and co and even when he was beaten he had luck on his side, a ferocious Jair effort rebounding safely off a post. Uruguay enjoyed rare sorties into Brazilian territory but they failed to trouble Barbosa in the Brazilian goal and there was no doubt that, even though the score was goalless at the break, it had emphatically been Brazil's half. Seconds after the start of the second period, it looked to be all over. Zizinho, who'd been kept relatively quiet all game by the close attention of wide defenders Victor Rodriguez Andrade and Schubert Gambetta, momentarily lost his marker Andrade and played the perfect ball through for Friaca, who kept his composure and guided the ball expertly past Maspoli and into the corner. 1-0 to Brazil and the crowd went wild, knowing only a miracle now could deny them. However, Varela was again to show his astute leadership and tactics. Despite knowing the goal was legitimate, he cleverly argued with referee Reader so as to slow the game down and allow the crowd to quiet down again. Eventually he strode back to his team with the ball and confidently stated: "Now it's time to win." With his unshakable belief and inspirational play on the pitch, Uruguay rallied and went on the offensive. The brilliant winger Alcides Ghiggia was again to the fore, tearing Brazil's left-back Bigode to shreds time and again as he worried him down the flank. It was Ghiggia who created the equaliser midway through the second period, pulling back for Juan Schiaffino to drill beyond Barbosa. Still, Brazil were champions if the score remained the same but the anxiety of the crowd filtered into the players as they retreated into desperate defending, very much against their style. The physical exertions of the tournament began to take their toll, while the fresher Uruguayans roamed about the pitch, Varela and Andrade utterly bossing the game in midfield. Brazil were hanging on but they received a sucker punch with ten minutes remaining. Ghiggia played a one-two with Julio Perez and again burst past Bigode. As he saw the defence rush to cover Schiaffino, Ghiggia surprised them all by instead shooting himself and beat the stunned Barbosa at his near post for 2-1. The dumbstruck crowd

> **Stat Attack**
>
> Uruguay winger Alcides Ghiggia set a new record for a player on a World Cup winning team by scoring in every game of the tournament, all the way to the final, a record since matched by Jairzinho. About his goal in the last game, Ghiggia later said: "Only three people have, with just one motion, silenced the Maracana: Frank Sinatra, Pope John Paul II and me."

went utterly silent and Brazil, shocked and shattered, could not respond. Incredibly, they had lost at the last and Uruguay had snatched the unlikeliest of victories. Still unbeaten in World Cups, they were world champions again.

> **Only at the World Cup**
>
> Brazil had been victims of their own overconfidence, with many newspapers proclaiming them champions prior to the game. There had even been a victory song composed which was never aired. Even World Cup creator Jules Rimet was caught out by Uruguay's unexpected victory, as the dejected hosts left him out alone on the field so that, without any fanfare, he had to seek out Varela and hand him the trophy!

> **Stat Attack**
>
> Brazil's defeat makes them one of only two of the eight World Cup winners not to have won the title on home soil, Spain the others. They were unable to erase that record when they hosted again in 2014.

Final Pool results

Brazil 7-1 Sweden
09/07/50 – Rio de Janeiro (Maracana)
Brazil: Barbosa, Augusto (c), Juvenal, Bigode, Bauer, Danilo, Maneca, Zizinho, Ademir, Jair, Chico
Goals: Ademir 17, 36, 52, 58, Chico 39, 88, Maneca 85
Sweden: K Svensson, Samuelsson, E Nilsson (c), Andersson, K Nordahl, Gard, Sundqvist, Palmer, Jeppson, Skoglund, S Nilsson
Goals: Andersson pen 67
Referee: Ellis (England)

Uruguay 2-2 Spain
09/07/50 – Sao Paulo (Pacaembu)
Uruguay: Maspoli, Andrade, M Gonzalez, Tejera, J Gonzalez, Perez, Varela (c), Schiaffino, Ghiggia, Miguez, Vidal
Goals: Ghiggia 29, Varela 73
Spain: Ramallets, Alonso, Parra, J Gonzalvo, M Gonzalvo, Puchades, Basora, Igoa, Zarra, Molowny, Gainza (c)
Goals: Basora 32, 39
Referee: Griffiths (Wales)

Brazil 6-1 Spain
13/07/50 – Rio de Janeiro (Maracana)
Brazil: Barbosa, Augusto (c), Juvenal, Bigode, Bauer, Danilo, Friaca, Zizinho, Ademir, Jair, Chico
Goals: Ademir 15, 57, Jair 21, Chico 31, 55, Zizinho 67
Spain: Ramallets, Alonso, Parra, J Gonzalvo, M Gonzalvo, Puchades, Basora, Panizo, Zarra, Igoa, Gainza (c)
Goals: Igoa 71
Referee: Leafe (England)

Uruguay 3-2 Sweden
13/07/50 – Sao Paulo (Pacaembu)
Uruguay: Paz, Andrade, M Gonzalez, Tejera, Gambetta, Perez, Varela (c), Schiaffino, Ghiggia, Miguez, Vidal
Goals: Ghiggia 39, Miguez 77, 85
Sweden: K Svensson, Samuelsson, E Nilsson (c), Andersson, Johansson, Gard, Sundqvist, Palmer, Jeppson, Mellberg, Jonsson
Goals: Palmer 5, Sundqvist 40
Referee: Galeati (Italy)

Sweden 3-1 Spain
16/07/50 – Sao Paulo (Pacaembu)
Sweden: K Svensson, Samuelsson, E Nilsson (c), Andersson, Johansson, Gard, Sundqvist, Palmer, Rydell, Mellberg, Jonsson
Goals: Sundqvist 15, Mellberg 33, Palmer 80
Spain: Eizaguirre, Alonso, Parra, Asensi, Silva, Puchades, Basora, Hernandez, Zarra (c), Panizo, Juncosa
Goals: Zarra 82
Referee: Van der Meer (Holland)

Sweden claimed third place.

Uruguay 2-1 Brazil
16/07/50 – Rio de Janeiro (Maracana)
Uruguay: Maspoli, Andrade, M Gonzalez, Tejera, Gambetta, Perez, Varela (c), Schiaffino, Ghiggia, Miguez, Moran
Goals: Schiaffino 66, Ghiggia 79
Brazil: Barbosa, Augusto (c), Juvenal, Bigode, Bauer, Danilo, Friaca, Zizinho, Ademir, Jair, Chico
Goals: Friaca 47
Referee: Reader (England)

	Pld	W	D	L	GF	GA	Pts
Uruguay	3	2	1	0	7	5	5
Brazil	3	2	0	1	14	4	4
Sweden	3	1	0	2	6	11	2
Spain	3	0	1	2	4	11	1

Uruguay won the 1950 World Cup.

Tournament awards

Golden Boot: Ademir (Brazil) – 9 goals
(Runners-up: Oscar Omar Miguez (Uruguay)/Estanislao Basora (Spain) – 5)

Best Player: Zizinho (Brazil)

Best Goal: Alcides Ghiggia (Uruguay) – Brazil scored some sparkling goals in the tournament but Ghiggia's in the final game matched ability with importance. After playing a slick one-two with Julio Perez, Ghiggia demonstrated classic wing play by skinning left-back Bigode and beating keeper Barbosa at his near post from an almost impossible angle. I bet Frank Sinatra and Pope John Paul II couldn't have done that!

Star XI:
Goalkeeper – Roque Maspoli (Uruguay)
Defenders – Victor Rodriguez Andrade (Uruguay), Erik Nilsson (Sweden), Schubert Gambetta (Uruguay)
Midfielders – Bauer (Brazil), Obdulio Varela (Uruguay)
Forwards – Alcides Ghiggia (Uruguay), Zizinho (Brazil), Ademir (Brazil), Jair (Brazil), Juan Schiaffino (Uruguay)

World Cup Great – Zizinho (Brazil)

Brazil has produced a staggering array of breathtaking attacking midfielders and deep lying schemers in its history and arguably it is the position for which Brazil is most known, ahead even of its collection of deadly strikers. The likes of Didi, Gerson, Zico, Falcao and Ronaldinho have all been lauded to the skies as all-time greats but there is still a significant following in Brazil that claims that their predecessor in the position for the national team, Zizinho, was the best of all. Certainly, he was the man responsible for popularising the position in the country and few of his successors have ever lit up a World Cup to the same extent as him.

Zizinho was born as Thomaz Soares da Silva in Rio in 1921. He first came to prominence as a replacement for another early great of Brazilian football, striker Leonidas, at Flamengo. Although Zizinho was a different sort of player to Leonidas he proved a worthy replacement as the Black Diamond went off to Sao Paulo. Able to play as an outright striker or as a winger but most comfortable slotting into an advanced midfield position just behind the forwards, the youngster soon became the team's star, dictating the play, creating and scoring goals and terrifying defences with his blistering pace and bewitching movement. During the 1940s, Zizinho was unquestionably Flamengo's star, helping his side to three successive state championships and only being prevented from starring at the World Cup by the Second World War.

Come 1950, the 28-year-old was to finally get his chance to make his mark on the world stage, when the World Cup came to his home country. However, coach Flavio Costa surprisingly chose to leave out his star playmaker for Brazil's first two matches and without him they struggled, unimpressive in victory over Mexico and in drawing with Switzerland. With no margin for error against Yugoslavia, Costa called for Zizinho and he did not disappoint. Brazil's star was instrumental in the 2-0 win, pulling apart the Yugoslavs at will and scoring a sublime and deserved goal to cap a fine individual performance. His best performances, however, would come in the final group stage. He was the architect of Brazil's astonishing demolition of Sweden and Spain by a combined score of 13-2. He served almost as a personal supply line to centre forward Ademir, giving him the quality service on which he thrived and was particularly deadly. However, despite his strike partner grabbing nine goals in the tournament and Zizinho only two, he was still deservedly the one singled out for particular praise, as it was he who created the chances for his team mates and was at the hub of their brilliant play.

However, everything went wrong for Zizinho and Brazil in the final match. Uruguay, recognising his importance, man-marked him with Andrade and Gambetta throughout the game and, although he set up Friaca to score, he was largely subdued as Brazil shockingly lost. As with all of that side, he was unfairly blamed for the crushing failure and was never the same player again. He was forced out of Flamengo that same year and frequently passed over for national team selection, including being left out of the squad for the 1954 and 1958 World Cups, though he finished with an international record of 30 goals in 53 caps. However, his later years did see some success, most notably at Sao Paulo in his late 30s, before retiring in 1962, aged 41.

Sadly, few outside of Brazil have heard of Zizinho, possibly as a consequence of the fact Ademir's nine goals in 1950 looks more immediately impressive. However, no-one could argue that Zizinho wasn't the real star of Brazil's exceptional 1950 vintage. Perhaps his true importance was not realised until a generation inspired by him went on to incredible success in the following decade, amongst them Pelé, who considered him the greatest player ever, once saying: "Zizinho was a complete player. He played in midfield, in attack, he scored goals, he could mark, head and cross." Indeed many in Brazil still put him right up with the likes of Pelé and Garrincha as one of the three greatest players the country has ever produced. For a country as rich in quality players as Brazil, that is high praise indeed.

World Cup Great – Ademir (Brazil)

In Brazil, Pelé is unquestionably the national hero. It is not only because of his ability but because he was the star of the team which first carried off the World Cup. Perhaps if Brazil had triumphed as expected on home soil in 1950, then his predecessor as the team's star striker, Ademir, might have been the darling of the country instead.

The young Ademir first made his mark at top Rio club Vasco da Gama, the club where he would spend almost his entire career, save for a short spell at Fluminense, another Rio side, in the late 1940s. Over his career he would lead his clubs to six state titles, a fantastic achievement. It was with the national side, however, that he gave his most famous performances.

Brazil, as hosts and boasting a formidable attacking team, were favourites to win the World Cup in 1950. Due to the Second World War, it was Ademir's first tournament and the devastating centre forward started making up for lost time. He scored the first ever competitive goal at the new Maracana stadium in Rio in the opening game against Mexico and would notch another goal later in the game. However, he would really hit top form when his chief creator Zizinho was restored to the side for the third game against Yugoslavia. Together with his provider and the tricky Jair, he was part of a formidable attacking triumvirate for Brazil and they set to work in destroying Europe's best. Ademir scored in the 2-0 win over Yugoslavia but it was just a warm-up for greater things. He was utterly devastating against Sweden, smashing in four goals and notching a further two against Spain to finish as top scorer with nine goals, the highest individual tally in a single World Cup up to that point. However, Brazil incredibly lost to Uruguay in their final game to cede the trophy to their conquerors. The country was in shock and it marked the end of Ademir's reign of terror in the national team. He would continue to play sporadically for Brazil until 1953, notching a devastating 32 goals in 39 appearances.

Ademir would play on for a further three years domestically before retiring from football in 1956. Defences across the country will have breathed a sigh of relief on that day knowing they would never again be tormented by one of the world's most deadly strikers of all time. Ademir's combination of devastating pace and acceleration along with his incredible trickery and high-speed movement with the ball made him an absolute nightmare to defend against and as a finisher he was almost unrivalled, genuinely two-footed, phenomenal in the air and equally capable of thundering in a 30-yarder or cheekily tapping through the keeper's legs. Indeed, Ademir was so good, some experts have suggested he was instrumental in the development of the back four, which Brazil first unveiled to the world in the 1958 World Cup. By the 1950s, most teams had switched from the old 2-3-5 formation to 3-2-5, dropping the centre-half back to play as a modern-day stopper and give greater security to the defence. However, even then Ademir proved nigh on unstoppable, leading some of his opponents to play an extra man in as a second stopper or an early form of the sweeper.

It speaks volumes for Ademir's ability that almost single-handedly his brilliance was able to produce what would soon be a worldwide change in tactics. Not even fellow Brazilian greats Pelé and Ronaldo can boast that and Ademir is right up there with the best of them as one of the greatest strikers ever to come out of Brazil.

After two World Cups where the Europeans had been virtually unchallenged, Brazil 1950 saw the South Americans fight back in convincing fashion. Brazil and Uruguay had comfortably been the best two teams in the tournament and the Europeans had suffered some horrible embarrassments. Sweden and Spain may have got to the final group but they were obliterated by Brazil in the most convincing fashion possible. England, meanwhile, had a debut World Cup to forget, losing shockingly to the USA and failing to get out of their group. Arguably, the only Europeans who could be truly proud of their performances were Yugoslavia, a revelation in their group and running Brazil desperately close for qualification.

Brazil had easily been the best side in the tournament but in the end complacency and one of the all-time great team performances had undone them. Without a doubt they had played the tournament's best football and in Zizinho and Ademir they had its two biggest stars but it all counted for nothing after their final defeat at the Maracana. The nation was heartbroken and, sadly, the players bore the brunt of the blame, many of them never being selected for the national team again and all of them bearing the scars of defeat for the rest of their lives.

Uruguay, in contrast, had secured a glorious triumph that no-one, not even themselves, could have predicted. The incredible heart and will to play to the finish exhibited by Obdulio Varela and his cohorts was nothing short of breathtaking in the final. Varela's immense self-belief filtered down to the rest of the players and, crucially, they played without fear, even when facing a massive and hostile crowd and a team who had swept all before them. There is no doubt, however, that Uruguay were massively helped by the chaotic schedule allowing them to play two fewer matches than their opponents, giving them extra reserves of energy when it really mattered, most crucially in the final 20 minutes against Brazil.

That was by no means the only mistake in FIFA's organisation of the tournament. Attempts in dealing with the huge travel distances had been botched horribly, leaving teams exhausted in the later stages of the tournament. Meanwhile, deciding the destination of the World Cup via a group stage seemed ridiculous, even though in the end FIFA had been bailed out by Uruguay winning it outright in the final game. These were mistakes that would have to be addressed the next time the tournament came around in 1954.

> **Only at the World Cup**
>
> One of the unlikeliest victims of the sorrow of defeat back in Brazil were the team's shirts! Brazil had played up to that point decked out all in white but the shirts were criticised for not being patriotic enough. By the time of the next World Cup, the Brazilian team would be wearing the famous gold and green known and loved the world over today. Let's hope South Africa, with their six-coloured flag, don't get any ideas post 2010!

1954: Switzerland

Qualification

39 Entrants.
Uruguay qualified as holders.
Switzerland qualified as hosts.

Group 1

Norway 2-3 Saar, Norway 1-1 West Germany, West Germany 3-0 Saar, Saar 0-0 Norway, West Germany 5-1 Norway, Saar 1-3 West Germany

	Pld	W	D	L	GF	GA	Pts
West Germany	4	3	1	0	12	3	7
Saar	4	1	1	2	4	8	3
Norway	4	0	2	2	4	9	2

West Germany qualified.

Group 2

Finland 2-4 Belgium, Sweden 2-3 Belgium, Finland 3-3 Sweden, Sweden 4-0 Finland, Belgium 2-2 Finland, Belgium 2-0 Sweden

	Pld	W	D	L	GF	GA	Pts
Belgium	4	3	1	0	11	6	7
Sweden	4	1	1	2	9	8	3
Finland	4	0	2	2	7	13	2

Belgium qualified.

Group 3

Northern Ireland 1-3 Scotland, Wales 1-4 England, Scotland 3-3 Wales, England 3-1 Northern Ireland, Wales 1-2 Northern Ireland, Scotland 2-4 England

	Pld	W	D	L	GF	GA	Pts
England	3	3	0	0	11	4	6
Scotland	3	1	1	1	8	8	3
Northern Ireland	3	1	0	2	4	7	2
Wales	3	0	1	2	5	9	1

England and **Scotland** qualified.

Group 4

Luxembourg 1-6 France, Republic of Ireland 3-5 France, Republic of Ireland 4-0 Luxembourg, France 1-0 Republic of Ireland, France 8-0 Luxembourg, Luxembourg 0-1 Republic of Ireland

	Pld	W	D	L	GF	GA	Pts
France	4	4	0	0	20	4	8
Republic of Ireland	4	2	0	2	8	6	4
Luxembourg	4	0	0	4	1	19	0

France qualified.

Group 5

Austria 9-1 Portugal, Portugal 0-0 Austria

	Pld	W	D	L	GF	GA	Pts
Austria	2	1	1	0	9	1	3
Portugal	2	0	1	1	1	9	1

Austria qualified.

Group 6

Spain 4-1 Turkey, Turkey 1-0 Spain
Play-off (in Italy): Turkey 2-2 Spain (Turkey won on toss of coin)

Turkey qualified.

> **Only at the World Cup**
>
> Goal difference had yet to be introduced as a factor to separate teams level on points, meaning a play-off and then the toss of a coin were the only ways to decide Turkey's tie with Spain. The Turks won the coin toss and qualified, taking the Spaniards' seeding, which would later have serious consequences for the tournament.

Group 7

Poland withdrew.

Hungary qualified.

94

Group 8

Czechoslovakia 2-0 Romania, Romania 3-1 Bulgaria, Bulgaria 1-2 Czechoslovakia, Bulgaria 1-2 Romania, Romania 0-1 Czechoslovakia, Czechoslovakia 0-0 Bulgaria

	Pld	W	D	L	GF	GA	Pts
Czechoslovakia	4	3	1	0	5	1	7
Romania	4	2	0	2	5	5	4
Bulgaria	4	0	1	3	3	7	1

Czechoslovakia qualified.

Group 9

Egypt 1-2 Italy, Italy 5-1 Egypt

	Pld	W	D	L	GF	GA	Pts
Italy	2	2	0	0	7	2	4
Egypt	2	0	0	2	2	7	0

Italy qualified.

Group 10

Yugoslavia 1-0 Greece, Greece 1-0 Israel, Yugoslavia 1-0 Israel, Israel 0-2 Greece, Israel 0-1 Yugoslavia, Greece 0-1 Yugoslavia

	Pld	W	D	L	GF	GA	Pts
Yugoslavia	4	4	0	0	4	0	8
Greece	4	2	0	2	3	2	4
Israel	4	0	0	4	0	5	0

Yugoslavia qualified.

Group 11

Peru withdrew.
Paraguay 4-0 Chile, Chile 1-3 Paraguay, Chile 0-2 Brazil, Paraguay 0-1 Brazil, Brazil 1-0 Chile, Brazil 4-1 Paraguay

	Pld	W	D	L	GF	GA	Pts
Brazil	4	4	0	0	8	1	8
Paraguay	4	2	0	2	8	6	4
Chile	4	0	0	4	1	10	0

Brazil qualified.

Group 12

Mexico 8-0 Haiti, Haiti 0-4 Mexico, Mexico 4-0 USA, Mexcio 3-1 USA, Haiti 2-3 USA, Haiti 0-3 USA

	Pld	W	D	L	GF	GA	Pts
Mexico	4	4	0	0	19	1	8
USA	4	2	0	2	7	9	4
Haiti	4	0	0	4	2	18	0

Mexico qualified.

Group 13

Taiwan withdrew.
Japan 1-5 South Korea, Japan 2-2 South Korea

	Pld	W	D	L	GF	GA	Pts
South Korea	2	1	1	0	7	3	3
Japan	2	0	1	1	3	7	1

South Korea qualified.

The Contenders

Austria
Belgium
Brazil
Czechoslovakia
England
France
Hungary
Italy
Mexico
Scotland
South Korea
Switzerland
Turkey
Uruguay
West Germany
Yugoslavia

The World Cup returned to Europe for the first time in 16 years in 1954. Switzerland, who had stayed neutral throughout the Second World War and thus avoided the devastation wrought over much of the continent, seemed a logical host for the tournament and certainly the country's small size would mean there would be no repeat of the shambolic travel arrangements of Brazil 1950. Thankfully, the ridiculous final group stage used in that tournament had been abolished in favour of a return to a more standard knockout system for the later stages of the tournament. Another plus point for the world was that the tournament would be the first World Cup which would be fully televised and available for the viewing delight of those thousands of miles away from the action.

However, there were certainly more than a few negative points in the organisation of the fifth World Cup, some of which were questionable at best. Of the 16 qualified teams, eight had been designated seeded teams, with two such sides placed in each group of four. Strangely, it was decided that, allegedly to reduce fatigue, there would only be two rounds of group matches rather than three, with the two seeded teams playing only the two unseeded teams and not each other, therefore giving the seeded sides a huge advantage. This was not the only deeply debatable decision made by FIFA, who also decreed that there would be extra time in all matches level after 90 minutes, even in the group stage. In addition to this, the idea of goal difference to separate teams level on points was yet to be introduced, meaning play-offs would be used for this purpose, increasing the fatigue FIFA was supposedly trying to minimise. This system had already proved to be flawed in qualifying, since Spain had been forced to play a third game against Turkey despite having a vastly superior goal average over two legs, losing the third game on the toss of a coin to surrender their place at the finals to the Turks. This match had also exposed yet another flaw in FIFA's system in that it had decided the eight seeds before qualifying but Spain, who had been one of them, had been eliminated and the Turks, hardly the cream of world football at the time, had somewhat dubiously taken the seeding in their place. All in all, the organisation left much to be desired once again. Nevertheless, with several fine sides present, the competition promised much.

Brazil were the most fancied side in Group One as well as being one of the seeded teams. The shock defeat to Uruguay in the final game four years ago on home soil had been a crushing blow to the country and they had reacted with wholesale changes, including a brand new strip mirroring the gold and green on the country's flag. Almost the entire team who had failed at the final step last time around had also been replaced but not at the expense of quality. In young midfielder Didi and electric winger Julinho they had players of the highest calibre while new full-back pairing Djalma and Nilton Santos promised much, both in defence and in attack. **France** had strangely been the second team seeded ahead of Yugoslavia, despite the Eastern Europeans having a much better World Cup record. The decision seemed all the more strange as it was no result of France's devastating form in qualifying, since the seedings had been decided before qualification started. Still, with the formidable wide pair of Raymond Kopa and Jean Vincent and the defensive ability of sweeper Robert Jonquet, they were a capable outfit. Certainly, their seeding seemed to endanger **Yugoslavia**, who would again have to come face to face with Brazil in order to progress. Silver medallists in the last two Olympic Games, they had a fine side all round, with the likes of Stjepan Bobek, Bernard Vukas and Branko Zebec all knowing the way to goal and the outstanding Vladimir Beara between the sticks. The final side in the group were **Mexico**, again flying the flag for North America but again looking to be well short of the ability of their opponents at this level. Keeper Antonio Carbajal would no doubt benefit from his experience of Brazil but the feeling was that he would again be a busy man.

Stat Attack

The 1954 World Cup saw two firsts: all matches were televised for the first time while all players were assigned a squad number for the whole tournament. The squad size for each team was also fixed at 22, where it would remain until 2002.

Only at the World Cup

FIFA's shambolic organisation of the 1954 World Cup led to some ridiculous decisions. These included the two seeded teams in each group not playing each other, all seeds decided before qualifying, extra time in all drawn games and play-offs to separate teams level on points rather than goal difference. Mad!

Group Two was headed up by overwhelming favourites **Hungary**, Olympic champions in Helsinki in 1952. The "Magical Magyars" as they were known had easily been the best side the world had ever seen over the previous few years, demonstrating bewildering ability and movement to tear their opponents apart, including twice thrashing England. Revolutionary coach Gustav Sebes and his counterpart at top club MTK, Marton Bukovi, had created a new formation employing nominal centre forward Nandor Hidegkuti as a deep-lying playmaker in what was effectively a 3-3-4 or occasionally even 4-3-4 formation (thanks to keeper Gyula Grosics frequently moving up to cover as a sweeper when his team attacked). Hidegkuti was far from the team's only star, however. Captain and striker Ferenc Puskas was considerd by many at the time the greatest player ever and with the likes of Sandor Kocsis, Jozsef Bozsik, Zoltan Czibor and Mihaly Lantos assisting him, Hungary looked simply irresistible. If anyone was to stop them, it was unlikely to be the other seed in Group Two, which was surprisingly **Turkey** after they had defeated Spain on the toss of a coin. First-time qualifiers, the Turks would have a major challenge on their hands, even with the significant advantage of not having to play the rampant Hungarians. Legendary keeper Turgay Seren, who had been the key figure in their shock victory over West Germany in Berlin three years earlier, would need to be at the top of his game, while deadly forward Lefter Kucukandonyadis would look to score the goals needed to seal progression. Their chances would hinge on repeating their victory over group rivals **West Germany**. Admitted back into the fold, this would be their first tournament since the country had been split in two and their chances had been hindered by the fact their lack of a seeding meant they would have to face Hungary. Still, freethinking coach Sepp Herberger at least had some talented players to work with, such as Kaiserslautern's veteran playmaker Fritz Walter and powerful winger Helmut Rahn. The group's fourth side were **South Korea**, only Asia's second ever entrant and nothing seemed to suggest they could do any better than the Dutch East Indies had in their humbling experience in 1938. With no experience of facing Europe's best, their opening game against Hungary threatened to be a footballing massacre.

Reigning champions **Uruguay** would take part in their first ever World Cup in Europe as one of the seeds in Group Three. Juan Lopez's side had still not lost a single one of the eight matches they had played at World Cups and retained the core of the side which had clinched that unexpected triumph in Brazil, amongst them captain Obdulio Varela, schemer Juan Schiaffino and powerhouse striker Oscar Omar Miguez. They would also be boosted by several new stars, such as darting winger Julio Abbadie and commanding centre-back Jose Santamaria. The group's other seeds were **Austria**, who themselves were one of the best sides in the world. The only team in the world who boasted a respectable record against Hungary, many believed a showdown with their neighbours in the final was more than likely. The Austrians would also be one of the most exciting teams to watch thanks to their uniquely attacking approach. While all the world's other teams had by this point switched to a stopper centre-back system with at least three defenders, generally in a 3-2-5 formation, Austria continued to deploy their star centre half and captain, Ernst Ocwirk, in a midfield role in a deeply outdated 2-3-5 system. Certainly they would leak goals but they would also attack with great numbers and menace. Both the other two sides in the group also looked to have a chance. **Czechoslovakia** had a fine reputation at World Cup level, though their current squad had no experience at the tournament. Nevertheless, they certainly boasted quality in players like young defender Ladislav Novak. **Scotland**, meanwhile, would compete at a World Cup for the first time, having declined to travel four years earlier. They, however, were a team of few stars, hardly a side of the vintage of years past, and they could struggle in so competitive a group.

Walter Winterbottom's **England** were the most fancied of the Group Four sides, seeded despite just one previous, and largely forgettable, World Cup experience. Stanley Matthews, at 39 years of age, was still a huge threat to defences and together with Tom Finney, Nat Lofthouse and Billy Wright he was part of a fine side. Nevertheless, they had twice been humbled by Hungary and were starting to realise they were no longer the best side in the world, as they had been for much of the first half of the century. Also seeded were **Italy**, who had won the tournament both times it had previously been held in Europe. There looked little likelihood of a repeat performance, however, as their side were still to fully recover from the Superga disaster five years before. Juventus legend

Giampiero Boniperti was a fine forward but they did not have an established first team and could well be vulnerable. That seemed like good news for hosts **Switzerland**, who had not been granted a seeding despite the tournament being held in their own country, making it considerably harder for them to progress. Austrian coach Karl Rappan, however, had a trick up his sleeve with his new "verrou" (bolt) system, which gave birth to the sweeper position by dropping back an extra man behind the defence for greater security, creating a 1-3-3-3 system which would later heavily influence Italy's infamous "Catenaccio" style. In players like the capable Andre Neury, he had men who could make his new system successful, while a host of skilful attackers, including Charles Antenen, Jacques Fatton and Josef Hugi, would also give the hosts a cutting edge. The final side were **Belgium**, the least fancied of the four. Henri Coppens was a fine striker but there were few others in the team with the quality to support him and there looked little chance of them progressing ahead of any of the other three sides.

Debutants: Scotland, South Korea, Turkey, West Germany

The Draw

Group 1
Brazil
France
Mexico
Yugoslavia

Group 2
Hungary
Turkey
South Korea
West Germany

Group 3
Austria
Uruguay
Czechoslovakia
Scotland

Group 4
England
Italy
Belgium
Switzerland

Venues:
Berne, Basel, Geneva, Lausanne, Lugano, Zurich

The Tournament – 16 June-4 July

Group Stage – First series

Four matches kicked off simultaneously to open the 1954 World Cup on June 16th. In Group One, **France** and **Yugoslavia** faced each other knowing the winner would have an excellent chance of reaching the next stage. Perhaps it was the fact that the Yugoslavs knew they would have to face Brazil in their other game that caused them to attack with greater urgency, knowing how important a result in Lausanne was. Starting stronger, they took an early lead when Milos Milutinovic kept his composure in the area to place an accurate shot into the far corner, past the groping dive of keeper Francois Remetter. Remetter would be called on several more times in the game as the Yugoslavs, clearly the better side, continued to lay siege to the French goal without further success. Nevertheless, the French had no answer going forward and had lost their opening game, putting their hopes of a place in the quarter-finals in serious jeopardy.

The other match in Group One was nothing like as tight as **Brazil** gave an early illustration of their title credentials by thrashing a limited **Mexico** side in Geneva. Finding their feet after 23 minutes of goalless football, the South Americans were rampant in the remainder of the first half, scoring four times. Powerhouse centre forward Baltazar set them on their way, driving home from the edge of the area. Brilliant orchestrator Didi soon doubled the Brazilians' advantage with a sublime free-kick before fellow forward Pinga scored twice in quick succession to compound the Mexicans' misery. At least the outclassed Central Americans kept Brazil down to just one goal in the second half but that goal was memorable. Darting right winger Julinho, brilliant all game, showed off his fast footwork, bamboozling two defenders on the edge of the area before unleashing a rocket of a shot from out wide which flew past the unfortunate keeper and into the top corner. Brazil had laid down an early marker that they would take no prisoners this time around.

> **Stat Attack**
>
> Despite their brilliant performances in the tournament, Brazil's people never forgave their 1950 team for losing in the final and many were continually overlooked for selection, shown by just one of that starting XI, midfielder Bauer, playing against Mexico.

Reigning champions **Uruguay** got off to the perfect start in Group Three with a comfortable victory in Berne over **Czechoslovakia**. They dominated throughout the game, with the wing skills of Julio Abbadie a constant worry to the inexperienced Czechs, but strangely it was not until the final 20 minutes of the game that they were able to turn their dominance into goals. Eventually, however, it was big Oscar Omar Miguez with a header and the crafty Juan Schiaffino with a free-kick who scored the goals late on to secure the 2-0 win. Uruguay had started their first European adventure in the perfect fashion.

Meanwhile, their fellow seeds **Austria** also got off to a winning start in Zurich, edging out **Scotland** in a much tighter game than the other encounter in their group. Dangerous striker Erich Probst put the Austrians ahead just past the half-hour and from then on they were forced to deal with a succession of attacks from the Scots. However, goalkeeper Kurt Schmied refused to be beaten and turned in an inspired performance to deny the spirited Scots, keeping them out to the end to finish 1-0.

The following day in Group Four, hosts **Switzerland** got their own World Cup adventure underway in Lausanne against **Italy**. They had the perfect start when the superb Robert Ballaman headed them into an unlikely lead. The crowd were delighted but their side were unable to hold their lead to half-time. The ever-dangerous Giampiero Boniperti, twice on target against Egypt in qualifying, equalised late on and the Swiss had it all to do in the second period. At one point, Lorenzi thought he'd put Italy ahead only for referee Viana to disallow it controversially. For the rest of the game, he was to be berated repeatedly by the Italians. However, surprisingly the Swiss sneaked a late winner, an accurate finish from striker Josef Hugi sending the crowd into pandemonium once again. The defeated Italians turned to their darker side late on, kicking out in frustration at their energetic opponents but to no avail. Switzerland had started their tournament with a bang while the Italians would have it all to do to progress.

> **Stat Attack**
>
> Hungary's 9-0 destruction of South Korea set a new record for biggest World Cup victory that would not be bettered until 1982, when the Hungarians broke their own record in demolishing El Salvador 10-1.

Group Two kicked off with an embarrassingly one-sided encounter in Zurich between an irresistible **Hungary** side and the minnows of **South Korea**. Captain and star forward Ferenc Puskas put the tournament favourites ahead after 12 minutes and from then on it was one-way traffic. Left-back Mihaly Lantos doubled the score with a powerful free-kick and a rapid double from Puskas' strike partner Sandor Kocsis made it 4-0 at half-time. If the Koreans hoped Hungary would be sated in the second period, they were proved emphatically wrong. Kocsis soon completed an easy hat-trick, winger Zoltan Czibor scored a sixth before deep-lying centre forward Peter Palotas added two more in quick succession. Finally, Puskas, the orchestrator of the carnage and its initiator, had the final word with his second goal and Hungary's ninth in an unprecedented annihilation. Hungary were clearly the team to avoid.

As the Korean keeper was repeatedly picking the ball out of his net, **West Germany** were showing the foolishness of seeding **Turkey** ahead of them by comfortably beating the World Cup debutants in Berne. Suat Mamat shocked the Germans with a goal in the opening minutes to put the Turks into a surprise lead but Sepp Herberger's charges quickly rallied to show their superiority. Speedy winger Hans Schafer equalised with quarter of an hour gone and although the Germans were unable to make further inroads before the break, they ran riot in the final 45 minutes. Berni Klodt fired them in front and big centre forward Ottmar Walter gave them a two-goal cushion with a third goal on the hour. Fellow striker Max Morlock, a Nurnberg legend, made sure of it late on with a fourth and the Germans would at least have a win to take into their meeting with the "Magical Magyars".

Back in Group Four, **England** contrived to throw away victory against a hard-working but hardly exceptional **Belgium** side thanks to defensive errors. Pol Anoul gave Belgium a shock lead early on in Basel but England were not to be deterred. Stanley Matthews, even at 39 years of age, was still a formidable attacking presence and it was the winger's sublime through-ball that gave England an equaliser, inside forward Ivor Broadis latching onto it and slotting home. England were on a roll and produced a superb second when centre forward Nat Lofthouse stooped to direct a phenomenal diving header past Leopold Gernaey. When Broadis tucked in a neat second midway through the second period the game looked over. However, Belgium fought back gallantly, Henri Coppens pulling one back before Anoul finished with aplomb to level at 3-3. However, the rules of the competition stipulated that an additional 30 minutes extra time would have to be played. Bolton Wanderers legend Lofthouse took immediate advantage to put England back

> **Stat Attack**
>
> The 4-4 stalemate between England and Belgium remains the highest scoring draw ever in the World Cup finals, equalled only when the USSR faced Colombia in 1962.

in front but again they were unable to hold their lead, Jimmy Dickinson this time the guilty man as his attempt to head the ball behind only found the back of his own net. England had drawn when they really should have won and they would need to beat Switzerland if they were to progress.

Group Stage – Second series

In Group Three, **Scotland**, who had lost manager Andy Beattie after their opening game loss, fell to a crushing defeat against rampant **Uruguay**. The world champions had far too move skill, pace and invention for the Scots and had it been a boxing match it would have been stopped long before the final whistle. Little left winger Carlos Borges showed quick footwork to open the scoring after 17 minutes, shimmying out of one tackle to work himself the space to smash past keeper Fred Martin. On the half hour, the Scots were further behind when an unfortunate deflection off a blocked shot fell to lurking centre forward Oscar Miguez, who took delight in ramming it into the roof of the net. In the second half, Scotland briefly threatened a revival, Roque Maspoli unable to hold a powerful shot but scampering to catch it just before it crossed the line. A minute later, Borges showed the Scots how to finish, bursting in from the left flank and blasting past Martin. This was the cue for fellow winger Julio Abbadie, dazzling all tournament, to show his skills, dribbling in off the right wing and showing the cheekiest of finishes to flick the ball into the corner with his heel. Uruguay were now at the very top of their game, with Juan Schiaffino brilliantly dictating the play from deep and the formidable attacking trio of Abbadie, Miguez and Borges linking up exquisitely with almost telepathic movement and passing. It proved far too much for the poor Scots and Borges soon completed his hat-trick, again tearing the right-back to shreds, bursting past him and slamming his shot home. Miguez got his second in similar fashion, charging into the box and finishing emphatically. At the death, there was still time for the electric Abbadie to score his second with another cheeky finish, bursting inside, comprehensively wrong-footing the advancing keeper with a sublime sidestep and casually slotting into the empty net. Uruguay had served notice that Hungary would have a firm rival as a potent attacking force.

> **Stat Attack**
>
> Scotland's 7-0 hammering at the hands of reigning champions Uruguay is their heaviest ever defeat.

Meanwhile, fellow seeds **Austria** also made light work of their opponents **Czechoslovakia**, hammering them 5-0 in Zurich. Forwards Ernst Stojaspal and Erich Probst put them 2-0 up with less than four minutes on the clock and the Czechs, disheartened, never threatened a comeback as they put in another poor performance. Probst completed a hat-trick midway through the opening period and with the game dead after just 25 minutes, they relaxed, although Stojaspal did add a fifth goal in the second half. Austria were comfortably through with Uruguay.

In Lausanne, **Brazil** and **Yugoslavia**, both victors in their opening games, sought qualification from Group One. The Yugoslavs were a fine side and far more resilient at the back than the feeble Mexicans, with the Brazilian attacks floundering on their skilful half-backs. In response, the Yugoslavs prompted to good effect and took a deserved lead just after the break when Branko Zebec fired home. The South Americans were not about to give up, however, and Didi again proved his quality with a technically perfect half-volley past Vladimir Beara to equalise. Extra time came and went and the score remained 1-1, safely seeing both sides through to the next stage.

> **Only at the World Cup**
>
> The decision not to use goal difference to separate teams level on points not only resulted in play-offs for second place but also meant Uruguay and Austria in Group Three and Brazil and Yugoslavia in Group One had to draw lots to decide who topped the group. In both cases, the team with the worse goal difference won.

Meanwhile, **France** were desperate for victory over **Mexico** in Geneva to revive their own hopes of reaching the quarter-finals. It started well enough, winger Jean Vincent cutting in off the left wing and firing past goalkeeper Carbajal. 1-0 became 2-0 in the opening exchanges of the second half when defender Raul Cardenas inadvertently directed another French effort past his own keeper. If the French thought the game was won, however, they were mistaken. Jose Luis Lamadrid put Mexico back in contention from close range soon after and when Tomas Balcazar equalised with five minutes remaining, it looked as if extra time would be needed. However, as France poured forward, they looked certain to score only for a flailing Mexican hand to block a goalbound shot on the line for a clear penalty. Raymond Kopa stepped up and smashed the ball into the top corner to give France a last-gasp victory. However, their celebrations were cut short as news filtered through of the stalemate in the other game, which eliminated them. France's efforts had been in vain.

The seemingly unstoppable **Hungary** side marched into Basel firing on all cylinders and smashed **West Germany**, who chose to rest several of their best players, no doubt believing they had no chance of victory and would be better off saving their players for a possible play-off. Sandor Kocsis put the "Magical Magyars" ahead from close range after just three minutes and the outstanding Ferenc Puskas expertly slotted home a second soon after, followed by playing through Kocsis exquisitely for 3-0. Alfred Pfaff pulled one back before half-time but Hungary only underlined their superiority after the break. They quickly hit another four goals past the Germans, the returning Nandor Hidegkuti scoring twice, Kocsis completing a second successive hat-trick and Jozsef Toth adding number seven. Helmut Rahn replied for West Germany but within a minute Kocsis had scored his fourth and Hungary's eighth, giving the striker an incredible record of seven goals in two matches. Richard Herrmann did score again for the Germans late on but their 8-3 humbling had shown their limitations as a side and only added to Hungary's considerable reputation. However, they had suffered one major blow as captain and star player Ferenc Puskas, the main inspiration behind both of their wins, injured his ankle when he was tackled recklessly by Werner Liebrich. He could well be absent for some of the tournament.

> **Stat Attack**
>
> Sandor Kocsis became the first man to score two World Cup hat-tricks. Only three others have emulated this, two of them also in one tournament and Gerd Muller also achieving the feat in successive games.

Elsewhere, **Turkey** recovered from their defeat by the Germans to hand **South Korea** a second successive hammering. After ten minutes, Suat Mamat put them ahead from close range after good work down the left wing and this would precipitate a flurry of goals. The pick of them was the second, Lefter Kuckandonyadis hitting a ferocious first-time volley from the edge of the area which flew past hapless keeper Hong Duk-Yung into the top corner. Suat scored his second soon after and Burhan Sargun added goal number four before half-time. Burhan scored twice more after the break for a hat-trick, the first from close range, the second driven powerfully in off the far post. Erol Keskin completed the scoring by slotting home with 15 minutes to play and South Korea had been utterly humiliated. Turkey had earned themselves a replay, which would be a repeat of their clash with West Germany.

> **Stat Attack**
>
> South Korea's disastrous tournament saw them concede 16 goals in just two matches, the highest number of goals ever conceded by one team in a single World Cup.

In Lugano, **Italy** recovered from defeat against Switzerland to convincingly beat **Belgium**. Egisto Pandolfini's penalty just before half-time gave them a slight lead at the break but they cut loose thereafter. Carlo Galli soon headed in a second before Amleto Frignani and Benito Lorenzi stretched the Azzurri's lead. Pol Anoul did pull one back for the Belgians but their limitations had been exposed. Italy, though, had earned themselves a play-off.

England, meanwhile, ensured they topped Group Four with a comfortable victory over hosts **Switzerland** in the capital Berne. They dominated the game against lethargic opponents, who were strangely muted given home advantage and their earlier victory over Italy. Jimmy Mullen and

Dennis Wilshaw scored the goals that booked England's passage through to the quarter-finals. The Swiss, meanwhile, would have to negotiate a rematch with Italy in a play-off.

First Round results

Group 1

France 0-1 Yugoslavia
16/06/54 – Lausanne (Olympique de la Pontaise)
France: Remetter, Gianessi, Kaelbel, Penverne, Jonquet (c), Marcel, Kopa, Glovacki, Strappe, Dereuddre, Vincent
Yugoslavia: Beara, Stankovic, Horvat, Crnkovic, Zlatko Cajkovski, Boskov, Milutinovic, Mitic, Vukas, Bobek (c), Zebec
Goals: Milutinovic 15
Referee: Griffiths (Wales)

Brazil 5-0 Mexico
16/06/54 – Geneva (Charmilles)
Brazil: Castilho, Djalma Santos, Brandaozinho, Nilton Santos, Pinheiro, Bauer (c), Julinho, Didi, Baltazar, Pinga, Rodrigues
Goals: Baltazar 23, Didi 30, Pinga 34, 43, Julinho 69
Mexico: Mota, Lopez, Cardenas, Gomez, Romo, Avalos, Torres, Naranjo (c), Lamadrid, Balcazar, Arellano
Referee: Wyssling (Switzerland)

Brazil 1-1 Yugoslavia (aet)
19/06/54 – Lausanne (Olympique de la Pontaise)
Brazil: Castilho, Djalma Santos, Brandaozinho, Nilton Santos, Pinheiro, Bauer (c), Julinho, Didi, Baltazar, Pinga, Rodrigues
Goals: Didi 69
Yugoslavia: Beara, Stankovic, Horvat, Crnkovic, Zlatko Cajkovski, Boskov, Milutinovic, Mitic (c), Vukas, Dvornic, Zebec
Goals: Zebec 48
Referee: Faultless (Scotland)

France 3-2 Mexico
19/06/54 – Geneva (Charmilles)
France: Remetter, Gianessi, Kaelbel, Marche (c), Mahjoub, Marcel, Kopa, Ben Tifour, Strappe, Dereuddre, Vincent
Goals: Vincent 19, Cardenas (og) 49, Kopa pen 88
Mexico: Carbajal, Lopez, Cardenas, Martinez, Romo, Avalos, Torres, Naranjo (c), Lamadrid, Balcazar, Arellano
Goals: Lamadrid 54, Balcazar 85
Referee: Asensi (Spain)

	Pld	W	D	L	GF	GA	Pts
Yugoslavia	2	1	1	0	2	1	3
Brazil	2	1	1	0	6	1	3
France	2	1	0	1	3	3	2
Mexico	2	0	0	2	2	8	0

Yugoslavia and Brazil qualified for quarter-finals.

Group 2

Hungary 9-0 South Korea
17/06/54 – Zurich (Hardturm)
Hungary: Grosics, Buzanszky, Lorant, Lantos, Bozsik, Szojka, Budai, Kocsis, Palotas, Puskas (c), Czibor
Goals: Puskas 12, 89, Lantos 18, Kocsis 24, 36, 50, Czibor 59, Palotas 75, 83
South Korea: Hong Duk-Young, Park Kyu-Chong, Min Byung-Dae (c), Park Yae-Seung, Kang Chang-Gi, Choo Young-Kwang, Chung Nam-Sik, Park Il-Kap, Sung Nak-Woon, Woo Sang-Kwon, Choi Chung-Min
Referee: Vincenti (France)

Turkey 1-4 West Germany
17/06/54 – Berne (Wankdorf)
Turkey: Turgay (c), Ridvan, Basri, Mustafa, Cetin, Rober, Erol, Suat, Feridun, Burhan, Lefter
Goals: Suat 2
West Germany: Turek, Laband, Posipal, Kohlmeyer, Eckel, Mai, Klodt, Morlock, O Walter, F Walter (c), Schafer
Goals: Schafer 14, Klodt 52, O Walter 60, Morlock 84
Referee: Da Costa Vieira (Portugal)

Hungary 8-3 West Germany
20/06/54 – Basel (St. Jakob Stadium)
Hungary: Grosics, Buzanszky, Lorant, Lantos, Bozsik, Zakarias, J Toth, Kocsis, Hidegkuti, Puskas (c), Czibor
Goals: Kocsis 3, 21, 67, 78, Puskas 17, Hidegkuti 50, 54, J Toth 73
West Germany: Kwiatkowski, Bauer, Liebrich, Kohlmeyer, Posipal, Mebus, Rahn, Eckel, F Walter (c), Pfaff, Herrmann
Goals: Pfaff 25, Rahn 77, Herrmann 81
Referee: Ling (England)

Turkey 7-0 South Korea
20/06/54 – Geneva (Charmilles)
Turkey: Turgay (c), Ridvan, Basri, Mustafa, Cetin, Rober, Erol, Suat, Necmi, Burhan, Lefter
Goals: Suat 10, 30, Lefter 24, Burhan 37, 64, 70, Erol 76
South Korea: Hong Duk-Young, Park Kyu-Chong (c), Han Chang-Wha, Lee Chong-Kap, Kang Chang-Gi, Kim Ji-Sung, Choi Young-Keun, Lee Seo-Nam, Lee Ki-Joo, Woo Sang-Kwon, Chung Kook-Chin
Referee: Marino (Uruguay)

	Pld	W	D	L	GF	GA	Pts
Hungary	2	2	0	0	17	3	4
Turkey	2	1	0	1	8	4	2
West Germany	2	1	0	1	7	9	2
South Korea	2	0	0	2	0	16	0

Hungary qualified for quarter-finals, Turkey and West Germany to play-off.

Group 3

Uruguay 2-0 Czechoslovakia
16/06/54 – Berne (Wankdorf)
Uruguay: Maspoli, Andrade, Santamaria, Martinez, Cruz, Ambrois, Varela (c), Schiaffino, Abbadie, Miguez, Borges
Goals: Miguez 72, Schiaffino 81
Czechoslovakia: Reimann, Safranek, Trnka, Novak (c), Hledik, Hertl, Hlavacek, Hemele, Kacani, Pazicky, Pesek
Referee: Ellis (England)

Austria 1-0 Scotland
16/06/54 – Zurich (Hardturm)
Austria: Schmied, Hanappi, Barschandt, Happel, Ocwirk (c), Koller, R Korner, Schleger, Dienst, Probst, A Korner
Goals: Probst 33
Scotland: Martin, Cunningham (c), Docherty, Aird, Davidson, Cowie, Mackenzie, Fernie, Mochan, Brown, Ormond
Referee: Franken (Belgium)

Uruguay 7-0 Scotland
19/06/54 – Basel (St. Jakob Stadium)
Uruguay: Maspoli, Andrade, Santamaria, Martinez, Cruz, Ambrois, Varela (c), Schiaffino, Abbadie, Miguez, Borges
Goals: Borges 17, 47, 57, Miguez 30, 83, Abbadie 54, 85
Scotland: Martin, Cunningham (c), Docherty, Aird, Davidson, Cowie, Mackenzie, Fernie, Mochan, Brown, Ormond
Referee: Orlandini (Italy)

Austria 5-0 Czechoslovakia
19/06/54 – Zurich (Hardturm)
Austria: Schmied, Hanappi, Barschandt, Happel, Ocwirk (c), Koller, R Korner, Wagner, Stojaspal, Probst, A Korner
Goals: Stojaspal 3, 70, Probst 4, 21, 24
Czechoslovakia: Stacho, Safranek, Trnka, Novak (c), Pluskal, Hertl, Hlavacek, Hemele, Kacani, Pazicky, Kraus
Referee: Stefanovic (Yugoslavia)

	Pld	W	D	L	GF	GA	Pts
Austria	2	2	0	0	6	0	4
Uruguay	2	2	0	0	9	0	4
Czechoslovakia	2	0	0	2	0	7	0
Scotland	2	0	0	2	0	8	0

Austria and Uruguay qualified for quarter-finals.

Group 4

Italy 1-2 Switzerland
17/06/54 – Lausanne (Olympique de la Pontaise)
Italy: Ghezzi, Vincenzi, Tognon, Giacomazzi, Neri, Nesti, Muccinelli, Boniperti (c), Galli, Pandolfini, Lorenzi
Goals: Boniperti 44
Switzerland: Parlier, Neury, Kernen, Fluckiger, Bocquet (c), Casali, Ballaman, Vonlanthen, Hugi, Meier, Fatton
Goals: Ballaman 18, Hugi 78
Referee: Viana (Brazil)

England 4-4 Belgium (aet)
17/06/54 – Basel (St. Jakob Stadium)
England: Merrick, Staniforth, Wright (c), Byrne, Owen, Dickinson, Matthews, Broadis, Lofthouse, Taylor, Finney
Goals: Broadis 26, 63, Lofthouse 36, 91
Belgium: Gernaey, Dries, Huysmans, Van Brandt, Carre, Mees, Mermans (c), Houf, Coppens, Anoul, P Van Den Bosch
Goals: Anoul 5, 71, Coppens 67, Dickinson (og) 94
Referee: Schmetzer (West Germany)

Italy 4-1 Belgium
20/06/54 – Lugano (Cornaredo)
Italy: Ghezzi, Magnini, Tognon, Giacomazzi, Neri, Nesti, Frignani, Cappello, Galli, Pandolfini (c), Lorenzi
Goals: Pandolfini pen 41, Galli 48, Frignani 58, Lorenzi 78
Belgium: Gernaey, Dries, Huysmans, Van Brandt, Carre, Mees, Mermans (c), H Van Den Bosch, Coppens, Anoul, P Van Den Bosch
Goals: Anoul 81
Referee: Steiner (Austria)

England 2-0 Switzerland
20/06/54 – Berne (Wankdorf)
England: Merrick, Staniforth, Wright (c), Byrne, McGarry, Dickinson, Finney, Broadis, Wilshaw, Taylor, Mullen
Goals: Mullen 43, Wilshaw 69
Switzerland: Parlier, Neury, Kernen, Eggimann, Bocquet (c), Bigler, Ballaman, Vonlanthen, Antenen, Meier, Fatton
Referee: Zsolt (Hungary)

	Pld	W	D	L	GF	GA	Pts
England	2	1	1	0	6	4	3
Italy	2	1	0	1	5	3	2
Switzerland	2	1	0	1	2	3	2
Belgium	2	0	1	1	5	8	1

England qualified for quarter-finals, Italy and Switzerland to play-off.

Play-offs

With no goal difference to separate teams locked together on points, two quarter-final spots would have to be decided by play-offs. In Group Two, **West Germany**, with their stars restored, bounced back from their Hungarian hammering to thrash **Turkey** for the second time. One of those returning, left winger Hans Schafer, had an inspired game and set up the first goal after just seven minutes, tearing down the left and crossing for Ottmar Walter to fire home. Schafer was on the scoresheet himself five minutes later, again bursting through and this time finishing powerfully beyond stand-in keeper Sukru. The Turks were given hope when Mustafa headed in midway through the half but another returning star, Max Morlock, restored the Germans' two-goal advantage before the break. Morlock scored twice more in the second period for a hat-trick, with Fritz Walter also getting in on the action and Schafer adding his second and Germany's seventh. Lefter did pull one back late on but West Germany were easy victors and deserving of their place in the quarters.

In Basel, **Switzerland** also achieved a second victory over opponents they had already beaten, in this case **Italy**. The Italians had struggled all tournament and the incisive Swiss, roared on by the passionate home crowd, had no problems in dismissing them. Josef Hugi powerfully put them ahead early on and Robert Ballaman clipped home in a crowded box early in the second period. Fulvio Nesti did briefly give Italy hope midway through the second half, heading in after a goalmouth scramble, but Switzerland would re-establish their dominance with two late goals, both created by the superb Roger Vonlanthen. First, tearing down the left, he squared for Hugi to slide in his second of the game. Then in injury time his silky running drew the keeper off his line and allowed him to find the onrushing Jacques Fatton to slot into the empty net. The hosts had deservedly progressed.

> **Only at the World Cup**
>
> Switzerland's victory over Italy was followed by a mass pitch invasion as the delirious home crowd rushed to congratulate their side. Even some of the police joined in!

Play-off results

Turkey 2-7 West Germany
23/06/54 – Zurich (Hardturm)
Turkey: Sukru, Ridvan, Basri, Naci, Cetin (c), Rober, Erol, Mustafa, Necmi, Coskun, Lefter
Goals: Mustafa 21, Lefter 82
West Germany: Turek, Laband, Posipal, Bauer, Eckel, Mai, Klodt, Morlock, O Walter, F Walter (c), Schafer
Goals: O Walter 7, Schafer 12, 79, Morlock 30, 60, 77, F Walter 62
Referee: Vincenti (France)

Italy 1-4 Switzerland
23/06/54 – Basel (St. Jakob Stadium)
Italy: Viola, Magnini, Tognon, Giacomazzi, Mari, Nesti, Muccinelli, Segato, Frignani, Pandolfini (c), Lorenzi
Goals: Nesti 67
Switzerland: Parlier, Neury, Kernen, Eggimann, Bocquet (c), Casali, Ballaman, Vonlanthen, Hugi, Antenen, Fatton
Goals: Hugi 14, 85, Ballaman 48, Fatton 90
Referee: Griffiths (Wales)

West Germany and Switzerland qualified for quarter-finals.

Quarter-finals

One of the most astonishing World Cup matches ever took place in the intense heat of Lausanne as hosts **Switzerland** looked to get one over neighbours **Austria**. With Austrian keeper Kurt Schmied suffering from heatstroke and the rest of his team lethargic in the oppressive conditions, the Swiss took advantage to score three times in the opening 20 minutes to the delight of the home crowd. First, the ball fell to Robert Ballaman on the edge of the area and he drove it powerfully beyond Schmied. Josef Hugi then quickly added two more, twice beating Schmied from close range to send the terraces into ecstasy. However, the Austrians, as was their custom, suddenly woke up and proceeded to score five times in less than ten minutes, even having the time to miss a penalty! Theodor Wagner kicked off the goalfest with an accurate shot from the edge of the area before winger Alfred Korner struck a phenomenal second from out wide on the left, thundering an unstoppable shot into the top corner. A minute later Wagner had a second in almost identical fashion to his first to equalise before Ersnt Ocwirk shot to put them ahead for the first time. Another scintillating move then ended in Korner, who also missed a penalty in this period, firing powerfully beyond Eugene Parlier for a score of 5-3. The highest scoring half in World Cup history was not quite finished, however, Ballaman scoring his second to bring the sides in with the score 5-4. The frantic tempo slowed somewhat in the second half as both teams attempted to deal with their exhaustion in the scorching heat. Wagner smashed in his third for a hat-trick but Austria were again pegged back when Hugi also notched his third, his powerful shot from the edge of the area taking a deflection off Gerhard Hanappi and eluding the groping Schmied. Nevertheless, at the end it would be the Austrians who emerged victorious and they would have one more goal to celebrate, Erich Probst running clear and lifting the ball over Parlier for 7-5. The Austrians were through but surely football was the real winner in this gripping contest.

> **Stat Attack**
>
> The 12 goals scored in Austria's meeting with Switzerland is a World Cup record for one game.

> **Stat Attack**
>
> Austria became the first team ever to come back to win from three goals down in a World Cup. Only Portugal in 1966 have since emulated them.

> **Stat Attack**
>
> Wagner and Hugi's three-goal hauls in the game meant the tournament saw eight hat-tricks, easily a record for a single World Cup.

Meanwhile in Basel, **Uruguay** and **England** sparred for a place in the semi-finals. The South Americans took an early lead when Julio Abbadie, again a constant menace, pulled across the face and Carlos Borges drove past Gil Merrick at the far post. Nevertheless, England were undeterred and set about getting themselves back in the game. Stanley Matthews may have been a grizzled veteran but there was life in the old dog yet and he tormented Luis Cruz down the right flank. It was Matthews who created the equaliser, beautifully playing in Nat Lofthouse to tuck past Roque Maspoli into the corner. England, now level, went in search of the lead and should have taken it when Maspoli spilt a shot from range at the feet of Dennis Wilshaw but he guided his shot wide. This was to prove costly as Uruguay took the lead before half-time. Captain Obdulio Varela strode forward and unleashed a shot on goal from range that Merrick somehow allowed past him, despite it being eminently saveable. Worse was to come for England and Merrick just after the break, Varela's free-kick finding its way to Juan Schiaffino, who drove it powerfully beyond the keeper. Still, Matthews refused to give up and his dazzling wing work inspired his troops and constantly worried the world champions. He saw his shot hit a post but fellow winger Tom Finney did pull one back soon after, stabbing home from close range after Maspoli had failed to hold a shot. Uruguay started to suffer a succession of injuries, with key trio Varela, Abbadie and Oscar Miguez all forced off. Nevertheless, even with this great advantage of numbers, England couldn't find the equaliser they so desired and Javier Ambrois finished them 12 minutes from time, firing home coolly. The reigning champions went marching on, while England, though defeated, could hold their heads high for the part they had played in the contest.

> **Only at the World Cup**
>
> Keeper Gil Merrick was made a scapegoat back in England for his poor goalkeeping in the defeat to Uruguay. He was just the first in a long line of unfortunates who would bear the brunt of England's disappointed public after World Cup failures!

The following day in Geneva, **Yugoslavia** looked to make their technical superiority count against unfancied **West Germany**. Surprisingly, however, the Germans were gifted an early lead when Yugoslav defender Ivan Horvat managed to head past his own keeper as he attempted to clear an attack. The Eastern Europeans were undeterred and set about forcing their way back into the match, with the superb Branko Zebec at the forefront of their best moves, but the goal had instilled confidence into the Germans. They bravely held out and, with five minutes remaining, scored a second very much against the run of play, big Helmut Rahn collecting the ball and firing powerfully past Vladimir Beara from the edge of the area. The Germans had sprung a surprise and had unexpectedly reached the semi-finals, where they would be easily the least fancied of the four sides.

At the same time, a shockingly violent and bad-tempered game was taking place between two of the tournament's most skilful teams, **Hungary** and **Brazil**, which would be dubbed the "Battle of Berne". Hungary, missing the injured Ferenc Puskas, moved Zoltan Czibor into the inside forward position and the move went down a tee as Czibor was exceptional in an almost impossibly rough match. Hungary burst into life early on, scoring twice in the first seven minutes. Nandor Hidegkuti set them on their way, the ball falling to him at the end of a goalmouth scramble and the MTK star smashing it into the roof of the net. Hidegkuti turned provider three minutes later, the deep-lying playmaker drifting in a cross to the far post which the onrushing Sandor Kocsis headed past Castilho. From then on, the massively talented Europeans decided to concentrate on systematically fouling the Brazilians in an attempt to slow the pace of the game down. They certainly succeeded in this and also in enraging the South Americans. One such foul, however, brought down Indio in the penalty area and Djalma Santos slotted home the resulting penalty. The game was really to spark to life, however, midway through the second period, when English referee Arthur Ellis awarded Hungary a penalty for what had looked more like a Hungarian foul than anything else. Mihaly Lantos fired home the spot-kick but the Brazilians were now even angrier. Julinho pulled a goal back with a sublime strike from range, the ball swerving viciously into the far corner, but Didi saw his effort hit the bar while Gyula Grosics was a colossus in the Hungary goal. Soon, violence broke out in appalling fashion. Mihaly Toth, repeatedly kicked, was forced to limp out the game on the wing. Then, an over-zealous tackle led to Jozsef Bozsik and Nilton Santos having a full-scale punch-up, for which both were dismissed, though in the end the police were needed to separate them. Brazil were soon reduced to nine men when Humberto Tozzi reacted to further provocation by kicking one of the chief instigators, Gyula Lorant. It could have been more had Ellis seen Djalma Santos repeatedly chasing Czibor, spitting and attempting to kick him whenever the referee wasn't looking. Then, with many having almost forgotten about the actual game, Kocsis made sure of Hungary's win at the death, again ghosting in at the far post to head in Czibor's cross. The final whistle was far from the end of the carnage, however; Pinheiro was struck by a bottle, allegedly thrown by Puskas, and the enraged South Americans stormed the Hungarian dressing room, leading to a mass brawl with any available weapon used. Poor Toth was left lying unconscious while all players would leave covered in cuts and bruises. Scandalously, FIFA washed its hands of the entire affair and not a single player received a suspension for their part in the melee. Referee Ellis would later say: "They behaved like animals. It was a disgrace." It was truly a dark day for World Cup football.

> ### Only at the World Cup
>
> The infamous "Battle of Berne" between Hungary and Brazil saw some shocking violence. Three players were sent off, two of whom had to be dragged off by police after fighting, while Djalma Santos carried out a personal vendetta against Czibor, attacking him whenever the referee was looking away! After the whistle, Pinheiro was left with a huge cut after either Puskas or a member of the crowd threw a bottle at him. The furious Brazilians responded by turning off the lights in the Hungarian dressing room and then invading it, attacking the players with bottles, boots and whatever else they could find! Toth was knocked unconscious in the battle while both teams were left nursing injuries. After that even Celtic v Rangers would seem a friendly and mild-mannered contest!

Quarter-final results

Austria 7-5 Switzerland
26/06/54 – Lausanne (Olympique de la Pontaise)
Austria: Schmied, Hanappi, Barschandt, Happel, Ocwirk (c), Koller, R Korner, Wagner, Stojaspal, Probst, A Korner
Goals: Wagner 25, 27, 53, A Korner 26, 34, Ocwirk 32, Probst 76
Switzerland: Parlier, Neury, Kernen, Eggimann, Bocquet (c), Casali, Ballaman, Vonlanthen, Hugi, Antenen, Fatton
Goals: Ballaman 16, 39, Hugi 17, 19, 58
Referee: Faultless (Scotland)

England 2-4 Uruguay
26/06/54 – Basel (St. Jakob Stadium)
England: Merrick, Staniforth, Wright (c), Byrne, McGarry, Dickinson, Matthews, Broadis, Lofthouse, Wilshaw, Finney
Goals: Lofthouse 16, Finney 67
Uruguay: Maspoli, Andrade, Santamaria, Martinez, Cruz, Ambrois, Varela (c), Schiaffino, Abbadie, Miguez, Borges
Goals: Borges 5, Varela 39, Schiaffino 46, Ambrois 78
Referee: Steiner (Austria)

Yugoslavia 0-2 West Germany
27/06/54 – Geneva (Charmilles)
Yugoslavia: Beara, Stankovic, Horvat, Crnkovic, Zlatko Cajkovski, Boskov, Milutinovic, Mitic, Vukas, Bobek (c), Zebec
West Germany: Turek, Laband, Liebrich, Kohlmeyer, Eckel, Mai, Rahn, Morlock, O Walter, F Walter (c), Schafer
Goals: Horvat (og) 9, Rahn 85
Referee: Zsolt (Hungary)

Hungary 4-2 Brazil
27/06/54 – Berne (Wankdorf)
Hungary: Grosics, Buzanszky, Lorant, Lantos, Bozsik (c), Zakarias, J Toth, Kocsis, Hidegkuti, Czibor, M Toth
Goals: Hidegkuti 4, Kocsis 7, 88, Lantos pen 60
Sent off: Bozsik 71
Brazil: Castilho, Djalma Santos, Brandaozinho, Nilton Santos, Pinheiro, Bauer (c), Julinho, Didi, Indio, Humberto Tozzi, Maurinho
Goals: Djalma Santos pen 18, Julinho 65
Sent off: Nilton Santos 71, Humberto Tozzi 79
Referee: Ellis (England)

Austria, Uruguay, West Germany and Hungary qualified for semi-finals.

World Cup Great – Stanley Matthews (England)

In an age where even players in their late 20s are routinely being written off as past their best, Stanley Matthews offers hope to veterans everywhere. The man who played in the top division of English football at the age of 50 showed everyone that class is very much permanent.

The son of a celebrated local boxer, the young Matthews was signed by hometown club Stoke City as a teenager in 1932. A right winger of unblemished skill and natural pace, he looked a tremendous prospect. He soon established himself as a firm fan favourite and made his England debut in 1934, scoring in a win over Wales. Throughout the 1930s, his reputation grew and grew as he starred for club and country. He became the hero of Stoke to such an extent that when he requested a transfer in 1938, there was such public outcry that he changed his mind and stayed on at the club.

Matthews' career was forced to take a break for several years due to the Second World War, as he chose to serve in the RAF. After a fallout with Stoke on his return, he signed for Blackpool in 1947. Many thought that at the age of 32 his best years were behind him but he proved his doubters wrong, easily enjoying the best spell of his career in the orange of his new club. So impressive were Matthews' performances that he was the first player to win the Football Writers' Association Footballer of the Year award in 1948. Two years later, he would travel, aged 35, to his first World Cup. It is safe to say that had the tournament been held in 1942 or 1946, Matthews, in his prime, may very well have taken the tournament by storm and been its indisputable star player. As it was, he was strangely played in only one game in 1950, which England would lose 1-0 to Spain to exit the tournament in the first round. He would have to wait four more years to show his real worth in the competition.

The finest moment of Matthews' long and glittering career came in the 1953 FA Cup Final, forever dubbed the "Matthews Final". He ran the Bolton defence ragged all game, his phenomenal dribbling and approach play being the key factor as the Tangerines recovered from 3-1 down to win 4-3. Even though Stan Mortensen grabbed a hat-trick, it was Matthews who was named man of the match.

The following year, even at the age of 39, he was electric in the 1954 World Cup, terrorising Belgium in the group and turning in a particularly inspired performance in the quarter-final defeat to reigning champions Uruguay. The legendary number seven was a constant thorn in the Uruguayans' side, creating endless problems and at times seeming to play his opponents almost single-handed. He would go on to play a starring role in a 7-2 demolition of Scotland the following year, providing five assists with his unstoppable wing play. He would play his last ever match for England in 1957, aged 42, the oldest man ever to play for England.

Matthews would receive deserved recognition for his outstanding career, winning the first ever European Footballer of the Year award in 1956 and being awarded a CBE the year after. In 1961, he returned to Stoke and, although he was now 46 years old, he was the inspiration behind the club winning the Second Division that season, winning the Football Writers' Association Footballer of the Year award for a second time. He would finally call time on a glorious playing career in 1965, at the grand old age of 50, the oldest player ever to turn out in the top tier of English football. Just before his retirement, he would receive a knighthood for his services to the game, the only player ever to receive the honour while still playing the sport.

Sir Stan died in 2000 at the age of 85 and greats ancient and modern paid their respects to the Wizard of the Dribble and rightfully so. No player has ever come close to Matthews' longevity. That he was still tormenting left-backs in his 50s was testament to his ability and determination. A true gentleman on and off the pitch, the world is a lesser place without the great Sir Stanley Matthews.

Semi-finals

In Basel, neighbours **Austria** and **West Germany** faced one another with a place in the World Cup final at stake. The Austrians were heavily favoured against a largely unheralded German side. However, Austria had introduced their regular first-choice keeper Walter Zeman ahead of Schmied, who had been dependable throughout the tournament. The move proved disastrous, as Zeman's decision-making left much to be desired in the match. German skipper Fritz Walter had an inspired game and he created the first goal, pulling across the face for Hans Schafer to drive home. Just after the break, it got even better for Germany, Walter swinging in a corner and Max Morlock powering home a header as Zeman stood motionless. Nevertheless, Austria were capable of waking from their slumber at any time, as they had against Switzerland, and they looked to be doing so when fantastic footwork from Theodor Wagner created an opportunity that was eventually finished by Erich Probst. However, the expected fightback never transpired. Austria continued to slumber and Germany were surprisingly ruthless in punishing them. Fritz Walter converted a penalty with aplomb for 3-1 before his younger brother Ottmar headed in his corner at the near post. Worse was still to come for Austria, as the Walter brothers helped themselves to another goal each. First, the hapless Zeman felled Fritz as he skipped past him and the captain dusted himself down and tucked away the spot-kick. Then, Zeman was caught horribly out of position attempting to meet a right-wing cross, the ball travelling over him and allowing Ottmar Walter to head into the empty net. Astonishingly, the outsiders had won by a crushing 6-1. Austria had been put to the sword, their overly attacking system proving horribly outdated. West Germany, to everyone's surprise, including their own, would play in the final.

One of the greatest World Cup matches ever was taking place at the same time in Lausanne. World Cup favourites **Hungary** came up against the incumbents **Uruguay**, who had no desire to relinquish their trophy and had an outrageously gifted side of their own. Sadly, several players on both sides would be absent, including the two captains. Puskas for Hungary was still not fit after injury, while Toth also was struggling after the trauma of his experiences in Berne. Meanwhile, Uruguay would also miss skipper Varela along with Abbadie and Miguez, all injured against England. In Miguez's absence, playmaker Juan Schiaffino was deployed out of position as a centre forward and he would go on to have a major impact on proceedings. First of all, however, Hungary got off to another blistering start. Zoltan Czibor volleyed them ahead in the first half and Nandor Hidegkuti doubled their advantage straight after half-time, flying through the air to score with a diving header at the far post. Many teams would have crumbled in the face of this onslaught but not Uruguay. They had famously come back to win in the final match of 1950 and Schiaffino again was to the fore. The veteran schemer played a perfect through-ball for Juan Hohberg to tuck beyond Gyula Grosics for 2-1. The Europeans were hanging on as Schiaffino was giving another exhibition of his skill. With time running out, the Penarol star played another exquisite pass for Hohberg, who rounded Grosics and kept his composure to fire past the defenders on the line and incredibly take the game into extra time. Then for a third time Schiaffino played through Hohberg, who was on a hat-trick, but this time his shot came back off the post. Hungary had received a huge let-off and they responded in the perfect fashion. Twice, Sandor Kocsis exploited his dominance in the air to head beyond Roque Maspoli and eventually eliminate the courageous Uruguayans. Hungary assistant coach Gyula Mandi succinctly summed up the game afterwards, saying: "We beat the best team we have ever met." Uruguay had certainly played their part in a phenomenal game between two genuinely great sides but it would be the Hungarians who would compete in the final. The trophy would finally be going somewhere other than Uruguay and Italy.

> **Stat Attack**
>
> Sandor Kocsis' double took him to 11 goals for the tournament, a record at the time and one of only three occasions a player has reached double figures in a single World Cup.

> **Stat Attack**
>
> This was Uruguay's first ever World Cup defeat, after 24 years and 12 matches.

Semi-final results

West Germany 6-1 Austria
30/06/54 – Basel (St. Jakob Stadium)
West Germany: Turek, Posipal, Liebrich, Kohlmeyer, Eckel, Mai, Rahn, Morlock, O Walter, F Walter (c), Schafer
Goals: Schafer 31, Morlock 47, F Walter pen 54, pen 64, O Walter 61, 89
Austria: Zeman, Hanappi, Schleger, Happel, Ocwirk (c), Koller, R Korner, Wagner, Stojaspal, Probst, A Korner
Goals: Probst 51
Referee: Orlandini (Italy)

Hungary 4-2 Uruguay (aet)
30/06/54 – Lausanne (Olympique de la Pontaise)
Hungary: Grosics, Buzanszky, Lorant, Lantos, Bozsik (c), Zakarias, Budai, Kocsis, Hidegkuti, Czibor, Palotas
Goals: Czibor 13, Hidegkuti 46, Kocsis 111, 116
Uruguay: Maspoli, Andrade, Santamaria, Martinez (c), Cruz, Ambrois, Carballo, Hohberg, Souto, Schiaffino, Borges
Goals: Hohberg 75, 86
Referee: Griffiths (Wales)

West Germany and Hungary qualified for final, Austria and Uruguay to third-place play-off.

World Cup Great – Obdulio Varela (Uruguay)

By the 1950s, most teams were responding to an increasing glut of goals from ever-more potent strikers by dropping their centre half back as a stopper to act as a third defender and man-mark the opposition centre forward. This meant the end of the old centre half, in many ways the equivalent of the modern-day holding midfielder, a powerful presence in defence but constructive in attack. Together with Austria's Ernst Ocwirk, the last, and greatest, of this kind was legendary Uruguay captain Obdulio Varela.

After making his debut in the top tier of Uruguayan football with Montevideo club Wanderers in 1938, Varela set about establishing himself as the heartbeat of the team for club and country. He earned his first international cap a year later and would go on to be an ever-present in the national team, who at the time were still among the most feared in the world. In 1943, he transferred to Penarol, one of the two giants of the Uruguayan club game. He soon set about turning them into the most dominant club side in the country and possibly even the continent. With fellow Uruguay stars such as Roque Maspoli, Alcides Ghiggia, Oscar Miguez and Juan Schiaffino his team mates at the club, Varela's dominant play and inspirational leadership helped this star-studded outfit realise their potential.

The Second World War meant Varela did not have the opportunity to take part in World Cups during his 20s but its return to neighbouring Brazil in 1950 allowed the 32-year-old, now captain of the national team, to show his abilities on the world stage. He did not disappoint. Varela was the heartbeat of the side which reached the final game against Brazil still in with a chance of the trophy, helped by the captain's late equaliser against Spain. It was in the Maracana, having to beat the hosts to win, that Varela delivered one of the all-time great individual performances. He famously delivered a rousing speech before kick-off urging his team not to be intimidated by Brazil and play their normal game. Even when Uruguay went a goal down, he again showed his astute captaincy by deliberately arguing with the referee so as to allow the crowd to quiet down and Brazil to lose their momentum. He then was the key figure in the revival, bursting forward and playing in team mates as Uruguay shockingly won 2-1 to claim the World Cup.

Varela was again at his brilliant best, even at the age of 36, in the 1954 tournament, Uruguay's first in Europe. He was again the captain and shining light as Uruguay marched into the semi-finals. They would eventually lose against a brilliant Hungary side but Varela was absent from that game with injury, along with several of his team mates. Indeed, some believe that Varela's incredible leadership and will to win would have changed the outcome of the game. The fact Varela never lost a World Cup game suggests some logic in this.

Varela played out his career at Penarol, retiring in 1955. His retirement was a massive blow to Uruguayan football and indeed they would never again reach the same heights Varela had taken them to. The Black Chief's combination of strength, skill and relentless determination made him a formidable player and one of the greatest captains of all time. A fabulously talented all-rounder, Varela was a fearsome presence in defence but also skilful in attack, creating and scoring goals regularly. Sadly, he is not particularly famous in Europe but Varela's peerless displays are deserving of his ranking among the very top tier of great players.

Third-place Play-off

The day before the final, **Austria** and outgoing champions **Uruguay**, two of the best sides in the world, faced other for third place. The Uruguayans, tired after their epic clash with Hungary, seemed largely disinterested, allowing Austria, desperate to erase the memories of their thrashing at the hands of the Germans, to win with little trouble. A penalty from Ernst Stojaspal put them ahead but Uruguay were level at half-time thanks to a powerful shot from Juan Hohberg. Nevertheless, the hungrier Austrian team did get the victory they craved in the second half, owing much to the misfortune of Uruguay's Luis Cruz, the defender inadvertently deflecting a cross past Roque Maspoli at his near post. In the final minutes, captain Ernst Ocwirk made sure of it with a fine individual goal, creating space for himself to drive home from the right side of the area. Austria had claimed the bronze, not that a tired and under-motivated Uruguay side cared.

Third-place Play-off result

Austria 3-1 Uruguay
03/07/54 – Zurich (Hardturm)
Austria: Schmied, Hanappi, Barschandt, Kollmann, Ocwirk (c), Koller, R Korner, Wagner, Stojaspal, Probst, Dienst
Goals: Stojaspal pen 16, Cruz (og) 59, Ocwirk 89
Uruguay: Maspoli, Andrade, Santamaria, Martinez (c), Cruz, Mendez, Carballo, Hohberg, Abbadie, Schiaffino, Borges
Goals: Hohberg 22
Referee: Wyssling (Switzerland)

Austria claimed third place.

World Cup Great – Juan Schiaffino (Uruguay)

Uruguay may be most famous for its uncompromising defenders but it has also produced a host of extravagantly skilled attackers. That Juan Alberto Schiaffino stands as the best of all of them and arguably Uruguay's greatest ever player is testament to his tremendous ability.

The young inside forward first came to prominence as a teenager in the dominant Penarol side of the 1940s, led by the great Obdulio Varela. Schiaffino soon emerged as the side's attacking general, playing a deep-lying role where he would drop back into the midfield to create opportunities for his team mates, his brilliant range of passing and his own fearsome goalscoring armoury frightening countless defences. Schiaffino made his international debut in 1945 at the age of just 20 and soon established himself as a key player in a formidable Uruguay side.

Schiaffino was one of the stars of Uruguay's surprise World Cup triumph in 1950. Playing as a midfield playmaker in coach Juan Lopez's revolutionary 4-3-3 system, which would become the national team's formation of choice for decades to come, he was at his dazzling best in the 8-0 thumping of Bolivia, scoring twice and setting up countless more for the trio of attackers in front of him. His finest moment would come in the final, scoring the equaliser in a sensational performance as Uruguay shocked hosts Brazil to come from a goal down to win 2-1 and claim the Jules Rimet Trophy.

The hugely talented schemer was at the top of his game the next time the tournament came around in 1954. Scoring against Czechoslovakia, he was at the peak of his powers as Uruguay destroyed Scotland 7-0. Despite not getting on the scoresheet, he was easily the man of the match, dictating the play from deep and releasing his darting team mates time and again. He would return to scoring ways in the quarter-final against England, his fifth World Cup goal. However, with Oscar Miguez injured, he was played out of position at centre forward in the semi-final against Hungary. He performed admirably in this role, twice providing assists to Juan Hohberg with brilliant passes, but it was not enough as Uruguay lost.

After the tournament, Schiaffino moved to Italian giants AC Milan for a then world record transfer fee of £72,000. He soon became the star of his new side, inspiring them to the European Cup Final in 1958 and scoring in the desperately unlucky extra-time loss to Real Madrid.

Schiaffino also turned out for the Italian national team during this period, earning four caps with his adopted nation. He would eventually leave Milan to end his career with AS Roma in 1960, retiring two years later. It was the end of the career of one of the greatest playmakers ever to take up the game. The slim Schiaffino was blessed with phenomenal vision and passing ability, allowing him to pull the strings from deep as well as using his dribbling skills and potent shooting to regularly put himself on the scoresheet as well. That he is widely considered the best player ever for a country that has twice won the World Cup and produced a host of greats speaks volumes for the ability of the brilliant Schiaffino.

World Cup Final

At the Wankdorf Stadium in Berne, more than 60,000 people came to watch what was widely expected to be the coronation of the mighty **Hungary** team as world champions. They had captain and star man Ferenc Puskas back in their line-up (though there remained doubts about his fitness), while they had already annihilated their opponents, **West Germany**, 8-3 in a group game. On the day of the final, the weather was dreadful, with heavy rain lashing the stadium, and this would have an impact on the game, as the Hungarians struggled to put together their renowned passing game in the horrific conditions. Meanwhile, in Germany such conditions were known as "Fritz Walter weather" and their captain and key playmaker soon began to have a big impact on the game. Nevertheless, as always, Hungary came roaring out of the blocks and were two goals up after just eight minutes. First, Sandor Kocsis saw his shot blocked but the rebound fell for Puskas to stab home. Then, a horrible mix-up between keeper Toni Turek and his defender Werner Kohlmeyer allowed Zoltan Czibor, back out on the wing, to steal in and roll the ball into the empty net. After conceding so calamitous a goal, Germany might well have collapsed but they forced themselves back into the game just two minutes later. Helmut Rahn fired in a cross-shot from the left that the Hungarian defence failed to deal with and Max Morlock stretched to touch the ball past Gyula Grosics. Incredibly, Germany were level eight minutes later. Fritz Walter swung in a corner, Hans Schafer challenged Grosics – illegally in the eyes of many – and the ball flew over both to Rahn, lurking at the back post, who smashed it in for 2-2. Stunned, Hungary poured forward, looking to restore their lead. However, Turek was in no mood to be beaten; three times he brilliantly denied the alert Nandor Hidegkuti and when he was finally beaten his goalpost came to the rescue. Amazingly, the Germans were still level at the break.

The Hungarians came out for the second half determined to reassert their dominance and they poured forward once more in the early stages. Turek twice saved superbly from Puskas before Kohlmeyer also atoned for his earlier error, throwing himself in the way of another Puskas shot and scurrying back to again block the Hungary captain's follow-up on the line. Still Hungary attacked but still to no avail. Kocsis ghosted in at the far post but his header came back off the crossbar,

Czibor's shot was again kept out by Turek and Hidegkuti wastefully fired wide on the follow-up. Then, utterly against the run of play, a rare German sortie ended in Hans Schafer being blocked off but the ball falling on the edge of the area for Rahn, who fired powerfully into the corner for 3-2. The stadium went wild. West Germany were five minutes away from World Cup victory. However, now Puskas finally found his scoring touch, racing onto Mihaly Toth's through-ball and slotting under Grosics. However, Welsh linesman Griffiths flagged for offside and the goal was disallowed. Many would later claim the decision was wrong, including many Germans, but nevertheless, the decision stood. In injury time, Hungary had one last chance, Czibor lashing the ball goalwards but Turek again saving brilliantly. Incredibly, the seemingly unstoppable Hungary team had fallen at the final hurdle and West Germany, hugely unfancied before the start of the tournament, had triumphed gloriously, thanks to their opportunism, the heroics of keeper Turek and a considerable slice of luck. The result remains the greatest shock in World Cup final history and arguably the greatest footballing shock of all time.

> **Only at the World Cup**
>
> 12 years before "They think it's all over", German commentator Herbert Zimmermann gave the most famous piece of German commentary, saying: "Rahn should shoot from deep; Rahn shoots; GOAL GOAL GOAL!!", followed by: "OVER, OVER, OVER, the game is over!!"

> **Stat Attack**
>
> Hungary's defeat in the final brought to an end their run of 32 games unbeaten, having not lost since May 1950. This remained the longest ever unbeaten run in the history of international football, until it was beaten by Spain 55 years later in June 2009.

> **Stat Attack**
>
> West Germany's 1954 side both scored (25) and conceded (14) more goals than any other champions past or present. This is in keeping with the 1954 tournament itself, which has the highest average number of goals scored each match (5.38), while Hungary's 27 goals in the competition is the most ever scored by one team in a World Cup.

> **Only at the World Cup**
>
> The 1954 final is still legendary in Germany, where it is referred to as "The Miracle of Berne". In 2003, a film of the same name was made based around it.

World Cup Final result

West Germany 3-2 Hungary
04/07/54 – Berne (Wankdorf)
West Germany: Turek, Posipal, Liebrich, Kohlmeyer, Eckel, Mai, Rahn, Morlock, O Walter, F Walter (c), Schafer
Goals: Morlock 10, Rahn 18, 84
Hungary: Grosics, Buzanszky, Lorant, Lantos, Bozsik, Zakarias, Czibor, Kocsis, Hidegkuti, Puskas (c), M Toth
Goals: Puskas 6, Czibor 8
Referee: Ling (England)

West Germany won the 1954 World Cup.

Tournament awards

Golden Boot: Sandor Kocsis (Hungary) – 11 goals
(Runners-up: Max Morlock (West Germany)/Josef Hugi (Switzerland)/Erich Probst (Austria) – 6)

Best Player: Ferenc Puskas (Hungary)

Best Goal: Julinho (Brazil) – In a tournament awash with goals, there were several worthy candidates for this position but the outstanding Julinho is the clear winner. His solo effort against Mexico was pretty special but he bettered it with an outrageously swerving long-range shot into the top corner against Hungary.

Star XI:
Goalkeeper – Gyula Grosics (Hungary)
Defenders – Jose Santamaria (Uruguay), Ernst Ocwirk (Austria), Mihaly Lantos (Hungary)
Midfielders – Jozsef Bozsik (Hungary), Juan Schiaffino (Uruguay)
Forwards – Helmut Rahn (West Germany), Fritz Walter (West Germany), Sandor Kocsis (Hungary), Ferenc Puskas (Hungary), Zoltan Czibor (Hungary)

World Cup Great – Sandor Kocsis (Hungary)

Hungary has produced an incredible number of prolific goal scorers during its time as an international footballing force. However, while his legendary strike partner Ferenc Puskas may have scored more goals, no other Hungarian can match the incredible strike rate of Sandor Kocsis, who managed a staggering haul of 75 goals in just 68 games for his country.

Kocsis first began to make his name as a teenager at Ferencvaros, winning the Hungarian League in 1949. A year earlier he had won his first international cap. In November 1949, aged 20, he scored the first of an incredible seven international hat-tricks, with Sweden the unlucky opponents. Kocsis transferred to army club Honved in 1950 and there he linked up with the core of the Hungarian side that would go on to dominate world football, including Ferenc Puskas, Jozsef Bozsik and Zoltan Czibor. He was an instant hit in his new surroundings, topping the goalscoring charts in 1951 and 1952, the latter seeing him crowned the top scorer in Europe as Honved carried off the title.

1952 would also see Kocsis and Hungary secure Olympic gold in Helsinki, the striker scoring six goals in the tournament as Yugoslavia were brushed aside in the final. The following year, he again was one of the stars as Hungary twice destroyed England. He was one of the most prominent of the "Magical Magyars" side which would go on to record an incredible run of 32 consecutive matches unbeaten.

Kocsis warmed up for the 1954 World Cup by again finishing as Europe's top scorer as he helped Honved win the title once more. In Switzerland that summer he was in top form. He became the first player to score two World Cup hat-tricks with a combined seven goals against South Korea and West Germany in the first round. He would then score twice in each of Hungary's next games, his goals carrying his side to victory over Brazil and Uruguay and into the final, where West Germany again would be the opposition. Sadly for Kocsis and Hungary, the Germans won an incredible match 3-2 and it would be the only game he would not score in. However, he finished the tournament with 11 goals, a record only Just Fontaine has surpassed.

The era of the "Magical Magyars" ended in October 1956 when a revolution in Hungary was brutally suppressed by the Soviet army. The Honved team were in Spain at the time playing Athletic Bilbao in the European Cup. Most of their side, including Kocsis, opted against returning home and instead sought new clubs abroad. After a season with Swiss side Young Fellows, Kocsis moved to Barcelona, where he joined up with fellow Hungarian stars Czibor and Ladislao Kubala. His new side, which also included brilliant Spanish playmaker Luis Suarez among others, reached the European Cup Final in 1961. Kocsis and Czibor were both on the scoresheet but Barcelona eventually lost 3-2 to Benfica. Kocsis went on to retire in 1965.

Kocsis was a complete striker and a huge handful to the opposition. His big frame and powerful strength made him a nightmare for defenders to contend with and he was blessed with adept finishing with both feet. However, it was his ability in the air that made him most feared and he was nicknamed "Golden Head" by his followers. That Kocsis was part of an all-conquering team of stars yet still is remembered for his own individual brilliance illustrates the level of ability of this deadliest of strikers.

The 1954 World Cup was a no-holds-barred thrill ride from start to finish. With an average of more than five goals a game, many of them outstanding, there was constant excitement. There were also several fabulously talented teams on show, in particular the outstanding Hungarians and the defending champions Uruguay, and plenty of memorable matches: Hungary and Uruguay's own epic semi-final, Austria and Switzerland's quarter-final goalfest, Brazil's group game against Yugoslavia and England's incredible 4-4 draw with Belgium all spring to mind but for sheer drama it was hard to beat the final itself. West Germany's comeback from two goals down to beat the seemingly unstoppable Hungarians is one of the greatest upsets of all time and was pure sporting theatre.

For West Germany, triumph was hugely unexpected, especially after their 8-3 hammering at the hands of the Hungarians in the group stage. Written off before the tournament, they had defied the odds to carry off the trophy. Certainly, they had been more than a little lucky, the Hungarians coming desperately close to scoring on countless occasions and Puskas' disallowed equaliser almost certainly actually onside. Allegations would also arise years later that the Germans had been injected with steroids at half-time. Indeed, many of their players did suffer from jaundice in the years to follow. Nevertheless, to begrudge a German victory would be incredibly harsh. For a country still recovering from the horrors of war and of Nazi rule, it was a ray of hope and glory that was a major factor in the German people recovering a sense of national pride again. For German history, it was a momentous moment.

However, the end result was that Hungary, one of the most talented sides of all time, were denied the trophy their phenomenal side so richly deserved. The phrase that history remembers only the victor is incredibly apt here, as the poor Hungarians' dominance of world football for more than four years was forgotten in the shock of defeat in the most important match of all. However, their brilliance had lit up the tournament in a way that arguably no other side before or since has ever achieved.

As for the rest, Uruguay, Austria, Brazil and Yugoslavia had all had their moments and had made the tournament a better place by their presence. Uruguay in particular had fought a superb defence of their title, taking the rampant Hungarians into extra time despite the absence of inspirational captain Varela. They had proven themselves a fantastically gifted side.

Nevertheless, despite all the glittering football on show, FIFA's organisation had again been shocking. The group stages had been botched horribly and changes would be needed for next time around. However, if the glorious football of 1954 could be reproduced, the world would be in for another treat.

Printed in Great Britain
by Amazon